Teaching Rhythm

New Strategies and Techniques for Success

by David Newell

Gavin —

Great catching up with you.

David Newell

Teaching Rhythm

New Strategies and Techniques for Success

by David Newell

kjos Neil A. Kjos Music Company, 4382 Jutland Drive, San Diego, California 92117

W54
ISBN-10: 0-8497-7754-2
ISBN-13: 978-0-8497-7754-7

Teaching Rhythm:
New Strategies and Techniques for Success

Table of Contents

Introduction **1-6**

Part One
The Rhythm Learning Sequence: Planning for Success..8-73
Two Major Problems 8
Two Foundational Principles 10
Step One: **Perform It** 13-19
   The "Automatic Warm-up 16
   The Warm-up Scale for String Players and Choral Students 18
Step Two: **Count It** 19-23
Step Three: **See It** 24-35
   Rhythm Flashcards 24
   A Drill that Combines Steps One, Two, and Three 28
   Manipulating the Flashcards 29
   Putting the *Flash* in Flashcards 30
   About Flashcards: Personal Reflections 33
Step Four: **Test It** 35
"But This Process Just Takes Too Long" 37
Step Five: **Understand It** 38-44
   Rhythmic Literacy 39
   Rhythmic Dictation 42
• The Rhythm Learning Sequence in Review 44
Language and Rhythmic Literacy: A Comparison 46
The Rhythm Learning Sequence: Conclusions 49
The Sequence and the Method Book 50-55
   • Planning and the Method Book 53
     • Planning Ahead Made Easy: Marking the Method Book 54
Beginning Lessons 55-58
     • Format for a 30-Minute Instrumental Class 56

• Teaching Rhythm in Performing Ensembles 58-61
  • Can Rhythm Be Learned Through Literature? 59
• The Process of Music Education in Performance Groups 62-71
     The Two Part Rehearsal: The *Lesson* and the *Literature*...............64
        The Lesson Segment: The Group Private Lesson 65
        The Literature Segment: The Literature Is Experienced 66
        The One-Way Bridge 67
        Teaching During the Literature Segment 69
     The Four Magic Words: An Assessment Tool for the Teacher 69
     Percentage of Time Devoted to Each Segment of the Rehearsal 70
     Significant Advantages of the Two-Part Rehearsal Format 71
  A Comparison of Elementary and Secondary Planning 72

Part Two

An Expanded Discussion of Step Five: *Understand It*
A New Look at an Old System 77-115

  A Self Test 77
  Your Test Results 78
  A Significant Problem 80
  Cut-Time (Alla Breve -- 2/2) 80
  The Good News! Quarter Notes Are NOT One Count! 86
  The Founding Principle of Rhythmic Notation 89-104
     Teaching Music's Algebra to Students 91
     Variable-Count Whole Note Melodies 94
     Half Notes 97
     The 30-second Cut Time Lesson 102
     Whole Note Durations in Students' *Other* Music 103
     Solving for X 104
  The Story of the Bottom Number: The Origins 105-115
     A Study to Validate the Theory 106
     Conclusions 108
     The Whole Note System 110
     Why the One-Count Note? 111
     The Derivation of Cut Time *(alla breve)* 112
     An Objection to This New Definition 112
     Conclusions 113
     Teaching the Traditional Meaning of the Bottom Number 114

Part Three

A Discussion of Counting Systems **118-142**
Rhythm's *Lyrics* 119
One, *and ONLY ONE*, Word or Syllable for Each Printed
Musical Symbol 121
A Counting Language Is Also A *Musical* Language 124
The Two Types of Counting Systems.................................126-131
   The "1-e-&-a" System 126
   A Final Note on this Particular Number Counting System 128
   The Recommended System...129
Bloom's Taxonomy of Cognitive Skills 131
Putting Rhythms Into Space 132-138
   ".... And Where is That?" 133
A Controversial Idea on Cueing 139
Final Thoughts on Counting Systems in Simple Meter 142

Part Four

Teaching Compound Meter **144-193**
The Two Meters: Simple and Compound 144-146
   Simple Meter...144
   Compound Meter 145
"Teaching 6/8 in six is teaching music unmusically" 147
Teaching Compound 6/8..148-176
   The Rhythm Learning Sequence
   Step One: **The Musical Magic of Mother Goose** 149
   The Rhythm of Childhood 153
   Important, Related Activity 154
   Step Two: **Count It** 158
   Step Three: **See It** 160
   Step Four: **Test It** 163
   Step Five: **Understand It** 165-176
      Compound Meter Notation Is Unnecessary 166
      The Power of the Dot 167
      The Family of Notes 168
      The Solution to the Problem of Notating
      Compound Rhythms 169
      A Comparison of Simple and Compound Notation 170

Defining the Word "Compound" 171
Composer's Dilemma: Simple or Compound Notation? 173
Is This 6/8 Piece in Six or in Two? 174
Duple and Triple Meter 175
3/4 Time: Simple or Compound 175
A Compound Meter Counting System 176-185
Defining the Word "Triplet" 177
Counting Systems Model Performance 177
Numbers NOT To Be Used in Compound Meter 178
Counting Sixteenths in Compound 6/8 179
The Meanings of Numbers in Compound Time Signatures 185
Rhythmic Literacy in Compound Meter 189

Part Five

Introducing Students to *Irregular* Meter **196-206**
Combining Meters 197
Fractional Time Signatures 198
Changing $\frac{3\frac{1}{2}}{4}$ Into A "Real" Time Signature 203
Counting Irregular Meter 206-209
The Recommended Counting System 207
Irregular Meter and the Conductor's Baton 209
Closing Thoughts on Counting Systems in Irregular Meter 209

Final Thoughts **210-211**
Acknowledgments **212**

INTRODUCTION

One of the most meaningful and unforgettable compliments I ever received came near the end of my thirty-year career as a middle school band director. Ms. Smith, one of the school's guidance counselors and a person with a fine musical background, approached me at the conclusion of a concert and, in a voice choked with emotion said, "I have attended countless middle school band concerts over the years, and I know what to expect from them, but your bands *really move me*." Wow! What a wonderful thing to hear! So much more important to me than if she had told me that she was impressed with the students' technical proficiency or their excellent posture and the like, but she said they touched her emotionally.

She concluded her comments with a probing question. "How do you get 7th and 8th graders to play with such a mature sense of musical expression?" I responded with something like, "We work especially hard on that aspect of our playing, Judy." What I was actually thinking, but didn't share with her because it most likely would have sounded arrogant, was quite different. I believed then, as I do now, that all successful teachers have a couple of things they do really well, many that they do adequately, and a couple of things that they don't do very well at all. I was certainly aware of some things that I didn't do very well at all, but one of the things that I genuinely felt that I did really well was getting students to play expressively. I honestly believed that this ability was a *gift* that had been bestowed upon me. I didn't really know how I did it. It was just something that I was somehow usually able to accomplish. It wasn't until a few years later that I came to realize that there was actually no mysterious gift involved in the process. It was really something quite simple and logical, the realization of which ultimately led to the writing of this book.

During the first part of my career, having my bands sight-read a piece was almost always a musical disaster. Students would get so lost that the resulting cacophony of sounds became hysterically funny to them and they would actually break out laughing. Although I didn't let them know it, this "making fun" of music really irritated me. In retrospect I realize that I was basically irritated by my own inability to teach them to sight-read. Specifically, what I had not been able to do very well at all was teach them to read rhythms. It certainly wasn't fingerings or incorrect dynamics that were causing the total breakdowns during sight-reading. It was the fact that students were so lost that they were on different counts, sometimes even in different measures all at the same time and, little wonder, it sounded horrible. Leaving the sight-reading rehearsal, I would mull over what I should do with the piece the next rehearsal. "I think I'll try to work out the Introduction first. No, wait. The Introduction is too hard. I know. The middle section is easier. I'll start in the middle and then work backwards to the Introduction, and finally work out the ending." And that's the way the rehearsals of the piece would proceed day after day until the concert -- helping small groups of students to figure out their parts, one small section of the piece at a time, before moving on to tackle the next problem.

Thankfully, during the latter part of my career, sight-reading produced drastically different results. Over the years the students had developed the ability to literally sight-read anything that I put in front of them, because they had become wonderfully proficient at independently reading rhythms. On the unusual occasion when a major rhythm error did occur, I would simply use what I came to call my *four magic words*. "Clarinets, measure 23; *'Look at the rhythm'!*" The clarinets would look at the rhythm, give me a knowing nod acknowledging that they realized their error, and the full band would continue on to the end of the piece. The clarinets had "magically" fixed the rhythm themselves. Leaving the rehearsal, I would think to myself, "The first thing we should do with this piece is explore its form so that the students understand why the middle section has to be played in such a different style." I didn't have to plan for any class time to teach the students their parts. They had sight-read them.

During that first part of my career, my concerts were basically demonstrations of students simply regurgitating the notes on the page. For those early bands, the pieces of music were like giant jigsaw puzzles, and it took so long to get all of the little pieces of the puzzle in place that there was very little time left to try to make meaning out of the resulting picture. Later, with rhythm virtually eliminated as a problem, the students were able to see the whole picture from the very beginning. Every minute spent on the music from sight-reading to the concert was spent turning the notes on the page into MUSIC. If I had known then what I know now and if I had not been concerned about sounding boastful, I might have responded to the guidance counselor's kind comments with something like the following: "Judy, I have discovered the most unusual way to teach rhythm, and that single discovery has afforded me the luxury of being able to spend all of my rehearsal time on those aspects of the music that "moved" you -- the expressiveness, the intonation, balance, blend, dynamic contrasts, style, and so forth. The concert you just heard was simply a reflection of what we do every day in the classroom." My gift to my students, it turns out, was not some mysterious ability to somehow get them to play expressively. It was discovering an amazingly successful, but simple way to teach rhythm, so that even the very youngest of them could understand and perform it at a level far beyond what I would have ever believed possible.

For those of you about to investigate and perhaps implement the method for teaching rhythm that is advocated in this book, there is one, absolute requirement --- a completely open mind, a blank rhythmic slate. To my knowledge, this is the most unique look at rhythm in several centuries of music teaching and learning. Many of the basic concepts that we all hold dear about rhythm will be severely challenged. Teachers who adopt this method will not only have their students occasionally playing and singing seven-count whole notes, three-count half notes, and the like, but they will also discover that it takes only about thirty seconds to teach students to fully understand, accept, and enjoy cut time! A simple method for teaching students to read and perform compound meter such as 6/8 in 2 beats to the measure will be introduced. The book will assert that teaching compound 6/8 is actually easier than teaching 4/4. Rather than waiting around for their teachers to tell them "how it goes," students will become rhythmically independent problem solvers. The rewards of these daring new approaches will be well worth it. So, fasten your seat belts, hang on, and enjoy the ride.

My First Year in the Classroom

I might very well have had a one-year teaching career, even though I actually loved almost everything about my first year in the schools. It was great to finally be getting a paycheck after all of those tuition checks. It was wonderful to stop being a student after seventeen years of formal education. The people I worked with were dedicated and sincere and friendly and encouraging, and we were all employed by a wonderful school system. But the thing that almost drove me from the profession that first year was RHYTHM. I simply could not get my students to understand it, and it really frustrated me. I optimistically entered the profession thinking that I might eventually become a pretty good teacher, but I soon discovered that I couldn't even get my students to play dotted quarters and eighths! I tried everything I knew and nothing seemed to work. I spent hours creating worksheets that I was certain would do the trick. I had my elementary students put *down/up* foot-tapping arrows under every note on full pages in their lesson books. Every whole note in 4/4 time had eight arrows written under it. There were so many arrows on the page, it's a wonder the students could see the notes. And I thought that would help! It embarrasses me to even think about it today. If

I knew where those students were now, I would apologize to them. Fortunately for them, it didn't take me too long to discover the real problem: I didn't really know much about rhythm and certainly had no clue about how to teach it. I had thought that because I could read, write, and perform rhythms myself, all I had to do was *tell my students what I knew*. Open your heads, kids, and I'll pour it in. I was teaching rhythm the way I was taught it by my teachers, who were teaching it the way they were taught it by their teachers, and so on. But it just wasn't working.

The thing that kept me in the profession for another twenty-nine years was a philosophy that I picked up somewhere and that I heartily advocate and endorse to this day. From those early days in my career, I genuinely believed that if there was something that my students did not understand, it was not their fault. It was mine. They were not understanding what I was trying to teach them because I simply did not know how to present it. They did not need to concentrate harder and study more. I needed to concentrate harder and study more.

I began to do some serious reading and, to my personal amazement, discovered that there has actually been a significant amount of research done over many, many years on how students learn music. I guess I never really knew that. I read Edwin Gordon's work and actually understood some of it. I delved into the work of Shinichi Suzuki and genuinely related to his concepts and principles. I then reread Gordon and understood more of it. I attended workshops and observed band rehearsals and classes taught by recognized experts, and I kept reading and learning and growing and becoming more hopeful that there was a solution to this problem. I took summer classes, attended more workshops, and read countless journal articles dealing with rhythm. Over time, I began to develop some rather unusual ideas of my own. I basically cleared my mind of everything I thought I knew about rhythm and started to look at things from the students' perspective. And I had the luxury of having a personal laboratory in which to test my new ideas -- my wonderful students. The end result of all this is the body of work being presented in this book.

I do not consider my experiences with the teaching of rhythm to be at all unique. The various methods that music teachers employ in an effort to rhythmically educate their students seem to largely ignore the research that exists. The knowledge is out there, but it's not getting into the classroom where it needs to be. As a department chair in the public schools and later as a college supervisor of student teachers, I was privileged to observe many fine teachers over the years. To this day, I regularly visit music teacher bulletin boards on the internet to read the rhythm questions and answers that are tendered. I just do not see strong evidence of rhythm teaching methods being employed that are based on the existing research. I lament that in so many cases, the people who are doing the teaching are not getting hooked up with the available knowledge. I also think that I may know one of the reasons for this critical disconnect. In my personal view, most music learning theories and their resultant teaching methods are written in language that is unnecessarily obtuse and confusing. Music teachers are some of the busiest, most overworked people in any profession. They simply do not have the time to sit down and wade through complex sentences with an open, unabridged dictionary beside them. Even if they did, many of the words they would be forced to look up would not be in the dictionary, because they are author-invented. I have purposely chosen to share what I have discovered about rhythm in what I hope is straightforward, plain language. In the process of writing this book, I have envisioned you and I just sitting down together and having a chat. I have imagined myself overhearing you and a friend discussing something about rhythm teaching, and when your friend has left the room, I have pulled up a chair next to yours and said, "Ya' know, I might be onto something with this rhythm teaching stuff. Would you like to hear it?" Of course, I'm hoping your answer is, "Yes."

There is absolutely no doubt in my mind that this plain, shoptalk approach to the art of teaching rhythm will draw criticism in some circles. I will most likely be accused of making rhythm teaching seem just too simple. When that criticism comes to me, I intend to smile politely and say, "Thank you."

******

All of this reminds me of one of my favorite education stories. It seems that someone once wrote a *How To Do It* article that described the step-by-step process of building a hammock. The piece was then given to various groups of professionals, who were asked to critique it for correctness, clarity, and ease of understanding.

The group of clergy who examined the article reported back that they thought it was very well written and clear in every way. In fact, they all felt that they could follow the instructions and successfully build a hammock. Their only suggestion for improvement was that the writer might consider adding a "moral to the story," so to speak. They suggested that the piece conclude with a paragraph stating that the purpose of building a hammock was to ultimately lie down on it, look up at the beautiful blue sky, and contemplate the wonders and mysteries of the universe.

The engineers who looked at the piece also felt that it was very well written and very precise, with instructions that were logically sequenced and easy to follow. They felt that the drawings were especially helpful. Their only suggestion was that there needed to be a disclaimer that stated that if the hammock was expected to hold more than 300 pounds, the dimensions of the lumber that provided the main support needed to be proportionally larger.

The group of education professionals who critiqued it had no suggestions, just a question:

"Couldn't we make it harder to understand?"

Part One

The Rhythm Learning Sequence: Planning for Success

Two Major Problems

Of the many separate skills that young musicians need to acquire, rhythm may well be the most troublesome. Embouchure, posture, breathing, bowing, diction, vowel placement, tone production, fingerings, and so forth are accomplished with relative ease when compared to the job of figuring out "how something goes." Far too many of our students participate for years in school music programs and still do not have the ability to accurately work out the rhythmic aspects of a piece of music on their own. They need our help. This reliance upon us results in rehearsals that are all too often a series of small group lessons -- for instance, teaching the band's 3rd clarinets their rhythm at measure 17, followed by the 2nd trumpets, the trombones, and on and on. This precious time spent helping our students with their parts is, unfortunately, time that could be better spent on intonation, phrasing, style, expression, and the like -- those things that turn *notes* into *music*. Perhaps even more importantly, the result is rehearsals that are often boring for individual students who are required to sit quietly without participating while we help first this section and then that section.

Boring rehearsals may well be more of a problem than most of us realize. In the late 1980's or early 1990's, the Women Band Directors' National Association (WBDNA) conducted a very interesting and informative study. They asked guidance counselors and other professionals not associated with the music department in 20 states to talk to students in grades 8 through 12, who had dropped out of band after at least one full year of participation. "Scheduling problems, too much time involved, didn't like the teacher" were some of the more frequently heard responses. But the number one reason given for dropping out of band? 52.8% of the students said, *"I was bored."*

How is that possible? We teach the most exciting and energizing subject in the curriculum. How could students be bored making music? Well, yes, perhaps we'll have to admit that it might be boring to start working on Christmas music in October, but in many situations it just seems to take the students that long to adequately prepare the pieces. Music prepared for adjudicated events and festivals takes even longer, and so students just have to learn patience while all the problems are worked out -- many of the problems being rhythmic. Musical nuance and refinement cannot be the focus of the rehearsal until all the pieces of the musical puzzle are in place, meaning that the right notes are being played or sung at the right times -- in other words, the rhythms.

Concert music is not handed out so far in advance of a performance date because it takes instrumental students that long to learn the fingerings! As a matter of fact, when brass and woodwind students have difficulty with fingerings, they can almost always solve their own problems, because we have taught them how to use a fingering chart. But most students have been given few tools to use to effectively solve their own rhythm problems. As a matter of fact, far too many of our students have learned just the opposite. Rhythm problems are not theirs to solve at all. We will eventually get around to showing them how their parts go. All that is required of them is patience and a lot of sitting beside the road until help arrives.

It is perplexing, to say the least, to try to understand how something so simple can be so difficult to teach. The sight-reading abilities of average 2nd and 3rd year student musicians are woefully behind their technical abilities. They can give excellent performances of sophisticated pieces that they know, but they can't accurately read at sight something much simpler. And the thing that they cannot read is almost always the rhythms. Many people would agree that the vast majority of all sight-reading errors are rhythmic. The problem appears not to be in the notational system itself. Most people who become skilled musicians realize that the system is simple, it is logical, and it is easy to understand. This is one of the reasons it can be so frustrating to try to teach. We know how simple rhythm really is, and yet so many students just don't get it!

Precisely what are the problems with rhythm? Is rhythm just one of those things that takes time to figure out? Is it really a case of "the light" finally coming on when the students are older and more mature and better able to grasp abstract ideas? Or could it be a case of teachers failing to employ a well planned out, systematic approach to the teaching of rhythm, one based on research and logic?

Parts One and Two of this book deal with the problems associated with the sequencing of instruction when introducing students to rhythms. A five-step *Rhythm Learning Sequence* is revealed that enables students to become excellent rhythm readers. Part Two takes a significantly more detailed look at the fifth and final step of that sequence -- *Understanding Rhythm*. Not until students have a clear understanding of rhythm theory can they become rhythmically literate and independent. Readers are urged to read Part One of the book before Part Two. The sequence is important. The materials in Part One show us how to produce students who can perform rhythms. Part Two shows us how to help students understand those rhythms they can already perform.

Two Foundational Principles

There are two conditions which must always be in place in order for the introduction and retention of rhythms to be completely successful. If at any time students are not successful in learning a new rhythm, either one or both of these foundational principles has been violated. They are of primary importance and will be referred to throughout the text.

> **Foundational Principle #1**
>
> Students must be given the
> luxury of being able
> to concentrate on only
> *one thing at a time.*
>
> **Foundational Principle #2**
>
> Students must be given the
> time necessary to
> *master* that one thing before
> being moved on to the next
> logically sequenced step in
> the process.

It is imperative that we plan our instruction in such a way that the thing that we intend for our students to learn is the *only* thing that they have to think about at that time. If a new rhythm is to be learned, it must be isolated in such a way that students can focus all of their attention on the new rhythm -- nothing else. Secondly, that one thing must be *mastered* before anything new is added, and the next step must be a logical extension of the one just mastered.

Assuming that these two foundational principals are faithfully adhered to brings us to the most important question of all. What follows what? How should a new rhythm be taught? What exactly is that first step that must be taught and mastered, and then what follows that? Is there *a sequence of experiences* that results in successful rhythm learning? Over the next several pages, a five-step *Rhythm Learning Sequence* will be carefully laid out. It will be immediately recognized that the individual steps of the sequence are not new. They are those things that we all do when we attempt to teach rhythm to our students. Unfortunately, however, many of us make the following mistakes:

(1) We do not plan our rhythm teaching experiences far enough in advance to allow mastery of each step in the sequence. Too often we have our students turn the page in their books to see a new rhythm and, because the students need to know the new rhythm in order to practice the new page, we present all of the steps in the rhythm learning sequence in five minutes. *Rhythm teaching requires planning!*

(2) We do not present the five steps in their logical, sequential order. Instead of starting with the first step and then moving on to the second, then the third and so forth, it seems that most of us begin with step number three. We then move around among steps two, five, and four. Finally, because it doesn't seem to be working, we revert to step number one, the step with which we should have started.

These three ideas of one thing at a time, mastery, and sequencing are not new concepts. As a matter of fact, many of them are quite old. Jean Jacques Rousseau (French, 1712-1778), in his book entitled *Emile,* advocated that children should learn from the natural sequence of first concentrating on experiencing things, then experimenting with them, and finally reasoning about them. Swiss educational reformer Johann Heinrich Pestalozzi (1746-1827), inspired by these revolutionary ideas, used Rousseau's *Emile* as the basis for a new method of educating the common children in his native land. Pestalozzi reasoned that, for centuries before the advent of schools for the general public were established, children had very effectively learned by first watching and listening, and then imitating their parents and elders. Pestalozzi believed that this natural sequence of learning was the most effective means available. Children needed to *experience* the thing to be learned before being shown any sort of a *symbol* that represented the learning. In his schools, Pestalozzi very well might have had his students experience the physical act of dividing a pile of 18 pebbles into three equal groups before introducing the mathematical symbols of $18 \div 3 = 6$ or $3 \times 6 = 18$. He would have introduced his students to the actual experience before showing them the abstraction of the experience -- *the thing before the sign.*

"Pestalozzianism" swept through Europe and was introduced to America in the early 1800's. Lowell Mason, thought by many to be the first public school music teacher in The United States, adapted Pestalozzi's ideas to the teaching of music. He set down his "Principles of the Pestalozzian System of Music" in Boston in 1830. Three of these principles can be directly related to the concepts of one thing at a time, mastery, and sequencing:

> *One thing at a time:* -- to teach but one thing at a time -- rhythm, melody and expression to be taught and studied separately, before the child is called to the difficult task of attending to all at once.

> *Mastery* -- in practicing each step of each of these divisions, until he is the master of it, before passing to the next.

> *Sequencing* -- to teach sounds before signs...

These concepts have been further developed and refined in the twentieth century by many notable music educators. The Talent Education Method developed by Shinichi Suzuki in Japan after World War II very closely adheres to the principals suggested above. Edwin Gordon's work with Learning Sequences is an extension of the work of Pestalozzi.

If children can't learn the way we teach them,
then we must teach them the way they learn!

Author unknown

THE RHYTHM LEARNING SEQUENCE

The Rhythm Learning Sequence that we will be examining consists of five steps. They are simply labeled as follows:

- **Perform It**
- **Count It**
- **See It**
- **Test It**
- **Understand It**

We will take a detailed look at each of the above steps, one at a time, through the eyes of the students in a simulated young band class taught by a Mr. Johnston.

Step One
Perform It

Introduce the new rhythmic figure by rote in phrases that are one measure in length. The use of the voice on neutral syllables *(du or tu)* is highly recommended. It is important that the learners be able to concentrate completely on the *sound* and *feel* of the new rhythm.

- Use the *aural/oral* approach --in the ear and out the mouth. "Listen and repeat after me; my turn, your turn."
- Students who can vocalize the new rhythm with the proper style and feel have an internalized model of the rhythm being introduced.
- In instrumental settings, when the learning is transferred to instruments, it is important that the "melody" be so familiar that it requires virtually no thinking -- for example, an already thoroughly well-memorized *Major Scale*.
  - √ The students need to concentrate just on the sound and feel of the rhythm -- not on fingerings, pitches, or written notation.
- The full measure of rhythm should be played or sung on each pitch of the scale.

14

One of the most important things for us to understand is that our students need to have considerable experience with new rhythms before they are ever asked to look at them in print. New rhythmic figures must be introduced by sound rather than by sight. Before they can relate meaningfully to the look of a new rhythm, our students must already be able to musically perform it. They must be able to associate the rhythm's look with a sound that is already a part of their rhythmic repertoire. This experiential groundwork for the subsequent introduction of the printed symbols must be laid well in advance of the time that students are first asked to turn the page and look at a new rhythm. *Successful rhythm teaching requires planning.* The first words out of our mouths when introducing students to new rhythmic figures ought to be "Listen!" -- not "Look!"

******

The band's method book will be introducing the new rhythmic figure of four sixteenth notes in 4/4 to the students in three to four weeks' time. Mr. Johnston, the teacher, has planned ahead and has decided that today is the day to introduce his students to the sound and feel of the new rhythmic figure. In the middle of the warm-up period, he asks the students to temporarily put their instruments on their laps and to *"listen and repeat."* He starts a gentle lap pat, which the students join.

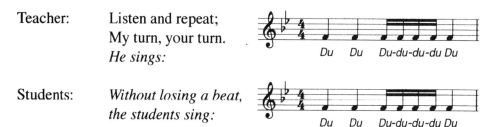

Teacher: Listen and repeat;
My turn, your turn.
He sings:

Students: *Without losing a beat,
the students sing:*

The beat continues and various other patterns follow.

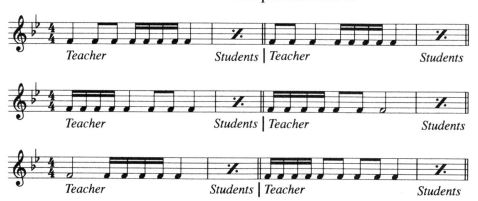

When he is satisfied that the students are singing the sixteenths with the proper style and feel and are patting their laps only once for the group of four sixteenths, he continues, keeping a steady beat going while talking:

Teacher: I want you to now transfer your lap pat to a nice, easy foot tap.* Good. Now pick up your instruments and continue to repeat after me, only this time, *play* the rhythms on a concert F. Ready? Instruments up. My turn, your turn.

The teacher sings and the students play the following rhythms on a concert F.

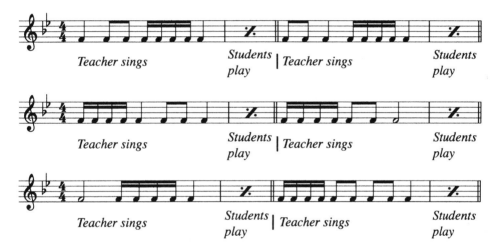

* Teachers who do not advocate having their students keep the beat by tapping their feet would substitute their own preferred method for achieving a steady beat.

As the students are performing the rhythm patterns, the teacher walks among them, making sure their feet are tapping only once for the groups of sixteenths.

Teacher: Good work. We'll do more of this next time.

******

The class continues without anything being said about the experience with these new rhythmic sounds. Step No.1 in the *Rhythm Learning Sequence* simply involves the students in the performance of the rhythm in the most natural way possible, by imitation. Music is, after all, an aural art. To the student who might ask, "Were those sixteenth notes?," the response is a simple, "They could be. It depends on the time signature. Don't worry about that for now. You'll understand it when you need to. All we need to do for now is learn to play them smoothly and evenly and make them sound like they're really easy. Just enjoy playing them!" The concentration is 100% on the *performance* of the new rhythm.

At every rehearsal over the next few days, two or three minutes at the most are spent with the same type of activity until the teacher is satisfied that the sixteenths are being performed musically and precisely.

It is during one of these early days of experience with the performance of this new rhythmic figure that the students' response is changed from the single pitch of Concert F. Doing a "listen and repeat" exercise on one constant pitch for more than a minute can become stiflingly boring and even irritating. To avoid this problem, the students begin playing the new rhythmic sounds on their "automatic" warm-up.

THE "AUTOMATIC" WARM-UP

In order to make the rhythms that our students are imitating sound a little more melodic, they need to be performed on different pitches. The entire measure's rhythm pattern must still be sung or played all on one pitch, but the pattern needs to be repeated on different scale degrees. When choosing what "melody" to have instrumentalists play, it is critical that "Foundational Principle No. 1" not be compromised. The melody must be so familiar and well-learned that the students do not have to give it a second thought. The fingerings and slide positions must be absolutely **automatic**, no conscious thought required. Students need to have the luxury of concentrating 100% on the sound and feel of the rhythm and nothing else.

The melody that first comes to mind when considering this in a band situation is the Concert Bb Major Scale. Because so many of the wind instruments in the band are pitched in Bb, this scale is considered by many to be the default band scale. This particular scale is only recommended, however, if the entire group can play it in "automatic" mode. In a very young band this could very well not be the case. For example, if any clarinetists in the group are still struggling with getting over the break, the Bb scale should definitely not become the automatic warm-up. Clarinet students approaching the break will not be able to concentrate on the rhythm. They will have to shift their concentration to their embouchures, their fingers, and their instruments, all the while worrying about the impending squeak that is waiting to "get them!" The same holds true for any brass players who may still be struggling with the range of the top two or three notes in the scale. None of these students will have *"... the luxury of being able to concentrate on only one thing at a time."*

In these cases, a partial Bb scale is strongly recommended for young band students. It consists of Concert F down to Concert Bb, four counts for each pitch. The sound is *sol, fa, mi, re, do* in Bb Major, as follows:

This partial scale offers several, significant advantages as the automatic warm-up for younger band students. These five notes are among the very first ones that they are introduced to in their beginning method books. Chances are good that this warm-up can, indeed, become automatic and require no conscious thought. Concert F is an excellent starting note for any rehearsal of young players. Many people recommend it over Bb as the tuning note for bands (except for oboes and Eb saxes, who should tune to Concert A). Being only five notes long, it does not take as long to complete a pattern as does the full octave Bb scale. If played all on one rhythm pattern, the eight pitches of the entire Bb Scale can themselves become too repetitive.

The five notes of this suggested young band warm-up should probably be the first thing that is played for the start of every rehearsal. Constant repetition is required in order for it to truly become automatic. After getting silence, we simply need to say "Let's warm up," and our band students should automatically play the five note partial scale as notated above, four counts each pitch. To the students, this five note pattern becomes known as *"The Warm-up."* And when, at any time in the rehearsal we say, "My turn, your turn" or "Listen and repeat," students should need no instructions concerning what notes to play. They know that these rhythmic echoing exercises are always played on their warm-up notes.

* * * * * *

Teacher: Instruments up. Listen and repeat. My turn, your turn.
             The teacher sings (or plays):

18

Without losing a beat, the students respond by playing:

When band students have advanced enough in their studies that all of them can flawlessly and effortlessly play the full Concert Bb Major Scale, then it can become the new warm-up.

Because Mr. Johnston's band class is being introduced to sixteenth notes in 4/4 time, it is likely that the student's are completely comfortable with the Concert Bb Major Scale. Therefore, as we continue to follow this particular class through the five steps of *The Rhythm Learning Sequence*, we will assume that the students have "graduated" to the full octave Bb scale from the five-note scale. The Concert Bb Major scale is their automatic warm-up.

Warm-up Scale for String Players
and Choral Students

An abbreviated warm-up scale is also advised for very young string students who are not yet competent in the performance of a full octave scale. It consists of four scalewise, ascending pitches, starting on the open D string: --- D, E, F#, and G, played for four counts each.

When the students demonstrate that they are capable of playing a full octave major scale as their automatic warm-up, the scale chosen should be the one with which they are the most familiar.

Choral students can sing the rhythm patterns on any scale or partial scale that comfortably fits into the ensembles' vocal range. Singing the scale using *solfege* or *du* is recommended. To avoid potential student confusion later on when counting rhythms is added to the process, choral teachers who use numbers rather than solfege to indicate pitches might consider employing a counting system that does not use numbers. The number "1" should not be used to indicate both the first degree of the scale and the first count in the measure.

It should be noted that the 4/4 rhythm patterns sung or played by the teacher of our hypothetical band class always end with a quarter note or longer. If they are to come in accurately on count one, students, whether instrumental or vocal, need time to process the rhythm. It is difficult for students to enter precisely on count one if the final count in a pattern is two eighth notes, and it is almost impossible if it is four sixteenths.

Mr. Johnston, whose students perform the complete scale as their warm-up, only perform the scale one octave in an ascending pattern. It is his thinking that he would rather have them experience two different patterns in about the same time that it would take to do one. Other teachers would probably have the students play the one given pattern both up and down the scale. Mr. Johnston is now satisfied that the sixteenths are being performed musically, easily, and accurately. In his view, the students have mastered Step One. It is time to initiate Step Two in the sequence.

THE RHYTHM LEARNING SEQUENCE
Step Two
Count It

Upon mastery of Step One in the sequence, the new rhythm needs to be presented with our individually preferred **counting names** (*1-e-&-a* or *Du-ta-de-ta* or *Ti-ri-ti-ri*, for example). This is best accomplished with the same simple and effective process of *Listen and Repeat*. Step Two has not been mastered until the students can flawlessly do the following:

When presenting the sound of $\frac{4}{4}$ ♩ ♩ ♬♬ ♩ |

The teacher intones: *Du Du Du-du-du-du Du.*
The students respond: *1   2   3 - e - & - a   4.*

Associating counting words with the sound of the new rhythmic figure of four sixteenth notes in 4/4 time associates a specific name with the new sound experience. This is a very important step in the process. Just as a computer file needs to be saved with a name attached, so that it can be located and isolated and worked with in the future, new rhythm sounds must also be saved as named files in the brain. At first glance it would seem logical that these new *du-du-du-du* sounds be named and filed away in a brain folder labeled "Sixteenths," but they cannot be. They are not sixteenth notes! They will not become sixteenth notes until they are seen. To date in the students' experience, they are simply new musical *sounds*, not new musical *symbols*. Students must not be allowed to teach themselves that words such as *1-e-&-a* exclusively represent the sound of four sixteenth notes. True, they are often the words that musicians associate with four sixteenths, but in 2/2 those same words represent eighth notes. Students who erroneously conclude that they exclusively represent the sound of four sixteenths will have a very difficult time accepting the fact that in other meters, those same words are symbolized by notes other than sixteenths. These new sounds are not sixteenths. They are *Du-ta-de-ta's* or *Mis-si-sip-pi's* or *1-e-&-da's*. That is why we have labeled this step *Count It* rather than *Name It*.

******

Once again Mr. Johnston begins his band class with the familiar listen and repeat activity, which is preparing his students for the upcoming unit on sixteenth notes in 4/4 time. It is important to remember that the method book unit on sixteenth notes is still a few pages in the future. For now, the students are simply being given the luxury of concentrating for a couple of minutes a day on the **counting names** of a new rhythmic sound they have yet to see.

Teacher: Listen carefully and echo me. Do exactly as I do.
                  He sings and the students echo sing, without missing a beat:

This is followed on the very next beat with the exact same rhythm pattern, but with new "lyrics."

The same sequence continues, without explanation. The teacher sings a pattern in the generic *du-du-du-du* language which, after the students' echo, is immediately translated into the teacher's preferred *1-e-&-a* counting names. The students are aurally learning their teacher's rhythm language. Languages are best learned aurally.

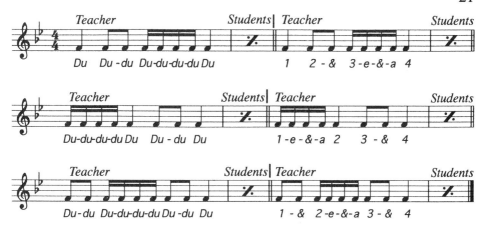

The students find this to be a very easy process. For a long time they have known their teacher's counting words for all of the rhythms they are hearing except for this newest rhythm that has four notes on one beat. They have but one new thing to learn -- the counting words that are associated with these new *du-du-du-du* sounds.

******

At this point in the sequence, it would be very tempting for Mr. Johnston to lecture his students on the theoretical aspects of this new rhythmic figure, forgetting that the students have yet to even see the notes. "These new notes that we have been doing are called sixteenth notes. Sixteenth notes are twice as fast as eighths. We all know that there are two eighth notes on every beat, one on the downbeat and one on the upbeat. If sixteenth notes are twice as fast as eighths, then there are two sixteenths on the downbeat and two on the upbeat. That is why we have to say four words for every count that has four sixteenth notes. And since we know that each eighth note is one-half of a count, then each sixteenth note has to be half of that, or one-fourth of a count," and so forth. Most of this is absolutely meaningless to the students and should not occur at this time. It most likely does more harm than good. Detailed, mathematical analysis of the rhythm is best delayed until students have spent more time getting comfortable with the sound, the feel, and the counting words of the new rhythm. Short explanations necessary to clear up any confusion are certainly necessary, but detailed analysis will very likely only confuse or turn students off. One of the reasons that music theory has such a bad connotation in the minds of many students is that theoretical explanations are offered before students have the experience necessary to make meaningful associations with the words being spoken.

Teachers telling students all about sixteenth notes before they have even seen them becomes a very *passive* experience for students. The word passive could very well be defined here as the state of "passing in one ear and out the other." **Telling is not teaching!** Student experience is the essence of education. Student learning is always far more profound and long term when students are given the time and the opportunity to *tell themselves* what they are experiencing. Students who are being introduced to the *1-e-&-a* counting language and who say to themselves, "Oh, I get it! Whether the *du-du-du-du* rhythm is called *1-e-&-a* or *2-e-&-a* depends on which count it's on. *Du-du-du-du* on count one in the measure is called *1-e-&-a*, but on count two it's called *2-e-&-a*. Yes!" For such students, the learning has become *active*, as in brain *activity*. Generally speaking, in music education we need to give our students more opportunities to figure things out on their own. The things that we learn most profoundly in life are those things that we tell ourselves rather than the things that someone else tells us. If students are correctly translating our *du-du-du-du* rhythms into *1-e-&-a's* or *3-e-&-a's*, they are getting it! They don't need any help from us. Detailed mathematical calculations and discussions only cloud the issue at this point in time. These are certainly important concepts that are necessary for total rhythmic competency, but not now! "Understand It" is Step Five in the sequence. We are only on Step Two at this point.

******

To date in Step Two: *Count It,* Mr. Johnston has used the aural/oral, listen and repeat approach to introduce his students to his preferred counting language. When he is certain that the students are totally at ease using this new vocabulary, he changes the focus to the most important aspect of this step in the sequence. Instead of just echoing him, he will now require them to think. The end goal of Step Two is for the students to be able to translate into **counting names** their teacher's presentation of the new rhythm on neutral syllables. Not until this association is accomplished will Mr. Johnston contemplate moving on to Step Three.

Teacher: Today for "My Turn/Your Turn," I will chant a rhythm
            pattern in *du-du-du-du* language, but you must respond
            immediately in *counting words*.

For example, if I say:

You must answer with:

Any questions? Here we go. *The teacher makes certain that the first rhythm is exactly the same as his example. This guarantees that every student will be successful as this new phase of Step Two is initiated.*

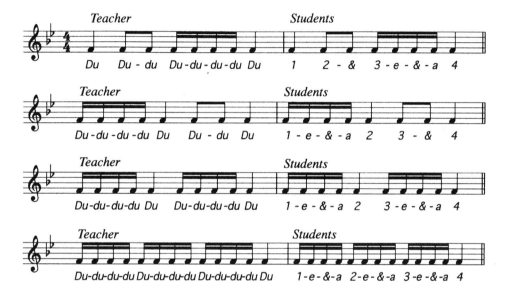

During these exercises, the teacher listens carefully for a solid, decisive, clearly articulated response from the class. He watches students' lips to try to make certain that they are all correctly associating the generic rhythm syllables with the correct counting names. Any rhythm pattern that does not receive a completely confident-sounding response is repeated. If necessary, time is taken to assess individual students' progress in cases where there may be a doubt. It is important that all students can correctly associate sounded rhythms with the appropriate counting names.

When the above kinds of exercises are being performed effortlessly and confidently by the students, Step Two has been mastered. It is now time for the students to actually see for the first time the musical symbols that are associated with the new rhythmic sounds they have been making. It is time for Step Three: *See It.*

THE RHYTHM LEARNING SEQUENCE
Step Three
See It

> With Step Three, it is time to show the learners for the first time *what the new rhythm looks like.* The goal is for the teacher to be able to say to the students, "This is the *look* of that rhythm you *can already do!*" If the sequence has been followed properly to this point, the learners are able to concentrate on only one thing -- what something that they do very well looks like. Measures of rhythm are best displayed on flashcards rather than the chalkboard, and they should initially be played or sung on a single pitch before being performed on a scale, one measure per pitch. Master this flashcard/chalkboard step before moving on.

The students in Mr. Johnston's class have been given the time necessary to master Steps One and Two of the *Rhythm Learning Sequence.* They now have the luxury of being able to concentrate on just one, simple thing -- the **look** of their newly mastered rhythmic sounds. Because Mr. Johnston is getting his students ready for the unit in the method book that introduces four sixteenth notes in 4/4 time, those are the kinds of notes and the meter signature that the students will initially be shown. A later lesson will have the students experience what the same rhythmic sounds look like in cut time.

To be the most effective, the rhythms are printed on flashcards rather than written on the chalkboard. Although the chalkboard can certainly be used to first expose students to the look of sixteenth notes in 4/4 time, flashcards are highly recommended. A detailed discussion of the many, significant advantages of flashcards will follow shortly.

******

Teacher: Listen and repeat after me. *The lesson begins with something totally familiar, a simple echo.*

Without stopping the beat, the teacher repeats the exact same pattern, except that as the students respond this time, he holds up a flashcard on which the measure is printed. The flashcard is large enough for the entire class to easily see. The teacher makes certain that he is far enough away from the class, so that the students on the sides of the room can see the flashcards as easily as the students in the center. There is no explanation relative to what the students are seeing, just the experience. As the students *say the words,* they *see the symbols.*

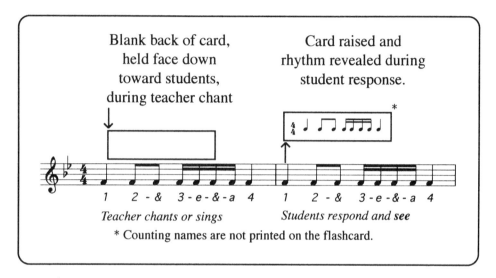

* Counting names are not printed on the flashcard.

This same measure is repeated a couple more times. The flashcard is held in place for the entire duration of the students' response, giving them ample opportunity to study the notational elements. The students have numerous, important things to tell themselves about the look of this new rhythmic figure.

Gradually the teacher changes flashcards and introduces different measures of rhythm, including measures that have the sixteenth notes on counts one and two, as well as on three. For now, the sixteenth are not placed on count four, because it is extremely difficult for the students to respond precisely on count one if the sixteenths are on four. The flashcards are always raised only on count one of the students' responses rather than during the teacher's presentations. During the teacher's chanting of the rhythm, the students see only the blank back of the card. This enables the more intellectually active students in the class to begin anticipating what the flashcard is going to look like before it is seen. The resulting intense student *brain activity* facilitates student learning that is more meaningful than even the most eloquently delivered "teacher words."

Each new measure is repeated at least twice, more if necessary. The card is always raised to reveal the notation on count one of the students' response. It is lowered, revealing the blank back of the card during the teachers' aural presentations, allowing students to concentrate on the sound of the rhythm before the sight of it.

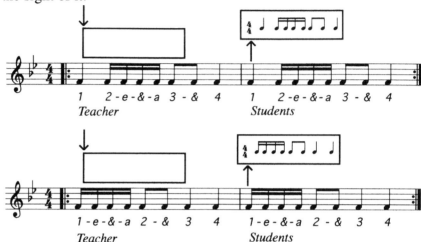

At the conclusion of this first "See It" session, the teacher and students summarize the experience. Not only does this bring closure to the day's lesson, but it is important for any students in the class who may not have totally understood it on their own. Additionally, students who have *told themselves* what they have experienced need verification that they have figured it out correctly. Any misconceptions need to be cleared up immediately. It should be noted that the explanations that take place during the discussion are following the experience, not preceding it. Students can directly relate what is being said to the musical sights and sounds that have just occurred. *Explanation follows experience!*

Among other things, the class concludes that:

- The new rhythm was introduced several classes ago as a four syllable counting word (*Mis-sis-sip-pi* or *Du-ta-de-ta* or *Ta-ka-di-mi* or *1-e-&-a*, and so forth). Therefore, it makes perfect sense that there are four notes in the written figure.
- The four notes in the new rhythmic figure have always sounded even. Therefore, it is logical that they all look even. In other words, they all look the same.
- The four new written notes resemble the students' old, familiar eighth notes, except that they are joined together by two beams rather than just one.

- Even before the students see the rhythm on the flashcard, they can tell whether the new rhythmic figure will be sitting on count 1, or count 2, or count 3, just by listening. They are establishing a solid foundation for the taking of rhythmic dictation later.

Teacher: I'll close this part of our class today by telling you what many of you probably already know. These new notes with two beams are called sixteenth notes. Let's see how many of you can remember that for next class. *The class moves on to the next part of their rehearsal.*

******

Flashcards can be either purchased commercially or can be "homemade." It is important that they be thicker stock than ordinary paper. Used manila file folders from the school office work very well. The folders need to be accurately trimmed to a uniform size and the notation neatly and uniformly written using a thick, black marker. Time signatures must appear on all flashcards. Make certain that the notation is large enough to be seen easily by all of the students in the room.

Excellent quality notation can be printed on 8.5x11 inch paper using most modern notation software programs. It is best that the notation be printed without staff lines, allowing students to concentrate totally on the rhythmic notation. Choose the largest notation size possible that will fit on one piece of paper, and print the measure in "Landscape" mode. Glue the paper onto the flashcard for stability and laminate it for durability.

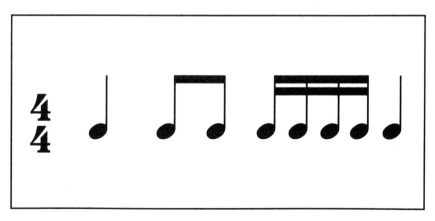

A Drill That Combines
Steps One, Two, And Three

Teacher:	Who remembers the name of the new notes we saw last class?
Several Students:	Sixteenth notes!
Teacher:	Right! *A short, verbal review of the last class follows. Review is important for all students, but especially important for any students who might have been absent last class.*
Teacher:	Let's do some. *The same flashcards and procedure from the preceding class are repeated for a very short period of time.*
Teacher:	Good! Now we'll change it just a little. I will chant a rhythm on neutral syllables like *du-du-du-du*, and you will say the same rhythm *twice* in counting words. For example, if I say *Du Du-du Du-du-du-du Du* (♩ ♫ ♬♩), you will say *1 2-& 3-e-&-a 4, 1 2-& 3-e-&-a 4*. Any questions? Let's try it.
Teacher:	My turn, your turn. *The flashcard is turned inward toward the teacher for the first two measures. Students see only its blank back side. It is turned up and its rhythm revealed on count one of the students' second measure and remains visible for the duration of the entire measure.*

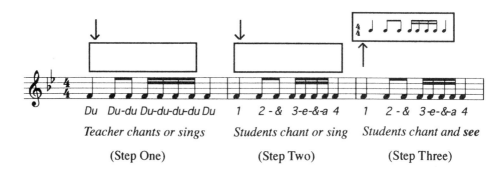

Du Du-du Du-du-du-du Du	1 2 - & 3-e-&-a 4	1 2 - & 3-e-&-a 4
Teacher chants or sings	*Students chant or sing*	*Students chant and **see***
(Step One)	(Step Two)	(Step Three)

Seeing that the students are successful with the procedure, the teacher utilizes his remaining sixteenth note flashcards. He immediately repeats any measures on which the students seem to hesitate. The entire exercise is done with a continuously flowing beat. After students finish the third measure of the previous exercise, the teacher chants the next rhythm on the next beat. After two or three minutes, the rehearsal moves on to the next planned event.

Manipulating the Flashcards

It would probably be a good idea to practice with the flashcards before trying the preceding exercise with students for the first time. As was recommended before, teachers who make their own cards should cut them uniformly into the exact same size. They need to be handled basically like a deck of large playing cards. This is very difficult to do if they are of assorted sizes. Once a set of cards is made, it might be a good idea to laminate them, as they will be used very often.

During these flashcard exercises, it is important that the beat continue unbroken throughout the displaying of all the measures of rhythm. This means that we need to know ahead of time what rhythm to chant next. To accomplish this, each card's rhythm needs to be handwritten on the back of the card in the lower left and/or right hand corner. The rhythms should be notated as small as possible, just large enough for the teachers to see. To further ensure that no students can read the rhythms during the time that students can see only the blank backs of the flashcards, the cards should be held by the lower left and right hand corners, making sure that a thumb or other part of the hand covers the small rhythm pattern written there.

Before beginning a flashcard exercise, the cards are held face down and tilted inward, so that students see only the blank back of the top card in our hands. The first rhythm chanted is the rhythm of the bottom card in the deck, which we have looked at and memorized beforehand. This bottom card is the one that the students will see when the cards are raised towards them. While the students are looking at the rhythm printed on this first raised card, we move our thumbs far enough to catch a glimpse of the small rhythm written on the back of the card that is now facing us. The deck of cards is lowered and, as we chant this new rhythm, we quietly shuffle the new card from the top to the bottom of the deck, so that when the deck is next raised, the new rhythm becomes the one that is seen by the students. The same "glance, lower, chant and shuffle" process continues until all the cards have been seen. Television often warns, "Boys and girls, don't try this at home!" We might say, "Teachers, you probably ought to try this at home!"

Putting The *FLASH* Into Flashcards

Up to this point in Step Three, the flashcards have been used only as a means of showing students the look of their new rhythmic figure. It goes without saying that the measures of rhythm seen so far could actually have been displayed on a chalkboard. However, chalkboards suffer from at least two important disadvantages when compared to flashcards.

- In doing the preceding exercises, several measures of rhythm would have to be written out in advance and visible on the chalkboard. This makes it difficult to ensure that every student in the class is focusing on the one, specific measure that is being considered at any given time.
- There is no practical way for us to control *when* and *for how long* our students see the rhythm. The importance of this will become apparent in the following, new exercises.

Before students can become competent rhythm readers, they must learn to see rhythms as *complete rhythmic ideas,* not as single beats. We often tell our students this, but as has been stated previously, telling is not teaching. When students read rhythms that are printed on a chalkboard or on a piece of paper, even if the last thing we say is, "See the notes as a complete idea, as a rhythmic phrase," there is no way we can be certain that our students are doing that. We need to employ a strategy that *forces* them to experience rhythms as rhythmic phrases. This is the important and distinct advantage of flashcards and is the next activity planned by Mr. Johnston for his students.

******

Teacher: Today I am simply going to show you some rhythms and I want you to say them for me one time in counting names. However, let me warn you. I am only going to show you the rhythms for a very short time. This is a test to see how quick you are! *Students love to be challenged this way. At a moderate tempo, the teacher says, "1, 2, Look and Say" to this rhythm* ($\frac{4}{4}$ ♩ ♩ ♫♩) *while manipulating the flashcards in the following manner:*

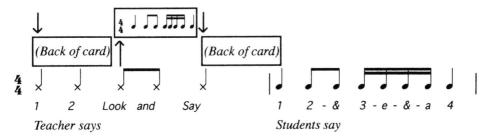

The flashcard is raised briskly on count three of the teacher's count-off measure, precisely on the word **"Look."** It is held steadily for the students to see during all of count three and is then lowered quickly on count four, on the word **"Say."** The students are forced to experience the rhythm as a complete pattern. They have no choice. They see the entire measure for less than one second, following which they have to immediately translate what they saw into rhythmic sounds. This obviously would not be possible if the rhythm had been written on the chalkboard or on a piece of paper.

The next logical step after several experiences with *"Look and Say"* is to have the students *"Look and Play"* each flashcard on a unison concert pitch. Once again, Mr. Johnston employs the "glance, lower, and shuffle" process described previously, thereby ensuring an unbroken beat and a variety of rhythms.

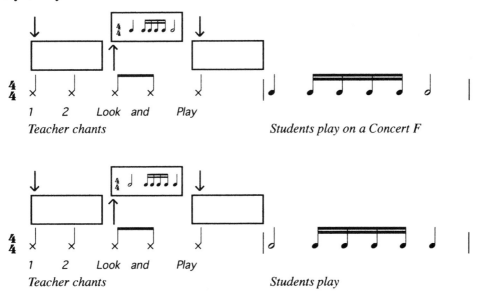

The final flashcard procedure that this particular teacher employs in Step Three is to have his students play the various rhythm patterns up the Concert Bb Major Scale. The first day the students play the entire scale on a single rhythm pattern. Next, the pattern is changed in the middle of the scale (on concert F) and finally, after much success with that, the students change rhythms every two measures, as demonstrated below. For variety, the teacher includes some measures that have no sixteenth notes. For those measures he includes older flashcards that were used when the students were first introduced to the looks of whole, half, quarter, and eighth notes. Notice, also, that sixteenth notes can now be placed on count four, as students have time in which to process the information.

Reminder: Both during the teacher count-off and as the students are playing, the flashcards are always raised briskly on count 3 and lowered precisely on count 4 in the measure before the new rhythm is to be played. The students are forced to grasp the entire measure in one, brief glance.

About Flashcards
Personal Reflections

I am indebted to one of my personal music education heroes, Dr. James Froseth of the University of Michigan, for introducing me to the use of flashcards. It was at one of his workshops many years ago that I first saw them used. After trying them out with my own band and general music students, I came to realize the phenomenal potential that they held. Of all the tools that I was able to develop and refine over the years in working with students, I rate rhythm flashcards very near the top in effectiveness.

First of all, they enable us to put into play "Foundational Principle No. One," that is, giving students "... the luxury of being able to concentrate on only *one thing at a time.*" When a rhythm flashcard is raised, all attention is right there where it needs to be. As has been stated previously, flashcards also give us complete control over when and for how long students see a rhythm. This is simply not possible if a large group of rhythm patterns is written out on either a chalkboard or on a piece of paper. An exercise like the one just described that has students changing rhythms every other measure forces students to (1) see the entire measure at a glance, and (2) store the new measure in memory for at least two counts. The students see the next measure's new rhythm while performing counts three and four of the old rhythm. Is this not what we are attempting to get our students to do when we tell them to *"look ahead?"* Instead of just telling students to look ahead in their music and to see rhythm groupings, flashcards enable us to force students to experience these two critical rhythm reading skills through performance. With frequent flashcard practice, students become especially adept at reading rhythms.

Flashcards ought to be used throughout the school year, not just during Step Three in the process of learning a new rhythm. Review rhythms using flashcards should be done on a frequent basis. The simulated band class that we are following as they are introduced to sixteenth notes in 4/4 has used flashcards to learn all of their basic rhythm patterns to date. This means that their teacher has a storehouse of flashcards embodying all of the following rhythmic elements in 4/4 meter: whole notes, dotted half notes, half notes, quarter notes, eighth notes, combination dotted quarters and eighths, and now sixteenths. As the students become more and more competent in the execution of sixteenth note rhythms, their teacher can begin to throw various review cards into the mix, making for some very interesting and challenging flashcard warm-up scale exercises.

34

But perhaps the best thing about rhythm flashcards is that *students love them*! Students enjoying important and essential drills is pretty hard to top in my view. As students become more and more competent at reading the flashcards, we can literally have students sitting on the edges of their chairs by gradually "raising the bar" in the following ways:

(1) We can shorten the time that students are given to see the cards. Instead of raising them on count three and lowering them on count four, the cards can be raised on the "and" of three and lowered on four.

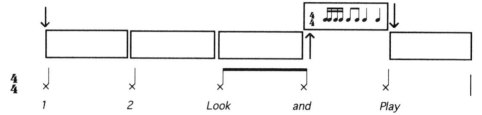

It is almost amazing how well students can do this and they will literally be on the edges of their seats!

(2) We can, with practice, change the flashcard *every measure* during a scale exercise, resulting in eight different rhythms for each playing of the scale. A new flashcard is raised every measure on count three, lowered on count four, and shuffled in time for the next count three. The next step would involve raising all eight cards on the "and" of three, as in the example above.

(3) As students become more advanced in their studies, we can have them perform flashcard scales utilizing cards with mixed meters. Groups that have learned compound meters, like 12/8 in 4 beats to the measure for instance, might do a rhythm exercise like the following:

    (a) Students go up the scale one time to four different cards in 4/4, changed every other measure.

    (b) We then switch decks of cards and have the students do the scale again, this time seeing four cards in compound 12/8.

    (c) As the students watch, we remove two cards from the 4/4 pile and two cards from the 12/8 pile.

We then shuffle the remaining four cards. Our students now know that they will be changing meters, but they don't know in what order the meters will be presented, nor do they know which specific rhythms have been removed.

(d) Advanced ensembles can do similar exercises using three or more meters and can be challenged to read cards that are changed every measure.

Note: Meters that have only two beats per measure, like compound 6/8, simple 2/4, or cut time require flashcards that have *two measures* written on them, so that teachers have time to change the flashcard on the third beat (count one of the second measure). Students should be instructed to always play *an entire flashcard* on one pitch of the scale. They should not change scale degrees at the barlines when doing flashcard exercises.

THE RHYTHM LEARNING SEQUENCE
Step Four
Test It

If Steps One, Two, and Three in the sequence have been successfully mastered, the learners ought to now be able to *generalize* the rhythm to new situations, such as published etudes or songs which include the rhythmic figure that is being studied. The learners should be able to visually recognize the new rhythm (step 3), call it by name -- in other words, count it (step 2) and perform it in an appropriate musical style (step 1). This fourth step, therefore, serves as an *evaluation tool*, allowing teachers to assess whether or not the learners are able to move from the known to the unknown as independent learners. If not, reteaching of the previous steps is required.

It is time for Mr. Johnston to **test** his students' learning relative to sixteenth notes in 4/4 meter. If they have indeed mastered Steps One, Two, and Three of the *Rhythm Learning Sequence*, they should be able to read at sight the first sixteenth note etudes from any published method book. In fact, the introductory sixteenth note etudes found in their books should be extremely easy for these students. The writers of the books composed the etudes as a way of introducing sixteenth notes to students who have never before seen or played them. With that in mind, they purposely made the etudes extremely easy. They wrote sixteenth note etudes for beginners. They didn't realize that Mr. Johnston's students were already sixteenth note experts. This is a good thing! Mr. Johnston's students begin the new unit with a positive and confident attitude about this "new" material. Their feelings of "This is really easy!" are so much more beneficial than the all-too-common "I don't get it."

It is important to note that the book's etudes contain sixteenth notes that are essentially identical in character to the ones that have been presented to the students prior to this point. That is to say, all four notes are on one pitch, for instance. Changing pitches anywhere within a group of four sixteenths is a separate skill that needs to be introduced later as an extension of their sixteenth note learning. The goal at this time is simply to evaluate whether or not students can successfully sight-read music that includes four sixteenth notes on one pitch in 4/4 meter. It is important that students be completely successful in their first attempt to read "real" sixteenth notes.

******

Teacher: Let's turn in our band books to start a brand new unit today. Page seventeen, please. Does anyone see anything on the page that you don't understand? *He waits and hears no questions.* Good. Instruments up, Let's play the first one. Ready, play.

******

After successfully completing a series of etudes like the one above, students will very quickly learn to play etudes in which the four sixteenth notes are not the same pitch, because that is not a rhythm problem. It is a coordination problem between the tongue and the fingers or slide positions or between the string player's left hand and the bow strokes. It is not something that needs to be taught. It simply needs to be practiced.

Students with a firm grasp of the basic rhythmic figure of four sixteenth notes in simple time signatures, find that variations on that pattern are also quite easily learned. The rhythmic figure of ♩ ♫ for example, can be introduced as "Double-Ups" -- two notes on the upbeats. Of course, all variations should first be performed and then counted before they are seen.

Two sixteenths on the downbeats can be taught as "Double-Downs."

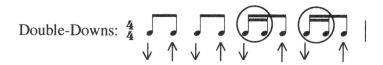

Assuming that "basic" syncopations (♩ ♪♩ ♪♩ ♩) have previously been mastered by students, ♩ ♫♩ can be taught as "syncopations on one count" --- first by sound and then by sight.

$$\frac{4}{4} \quad ♪♩ \quad ♪♩ \quad ♩ \quad | \quad ♫♩ \quad ♫♩ \quad ♫ \quad ♩ \quad |$$

Teaching the various mutations of basic rhythmic figures goes very quickly, because the students have mastered the fundamental rhythm from which the variations evolved.

"But This Process Just Takes Too Long!"

On the first reading of this material, it may appear to many that this *Rhythm Learning Sequence* as outlined thus far just takes too long to get through. There is so much for our students to accomplish and not nearly enough class time in which to get it all done! It needs to be emphatically stated here that *there are some things for which time must simply be taken.* Keep in mind that these "rhythm lessons" are most often taking only two to three minutes per class meeting. In the long run, the sequence actually saves an enormous amount of time. Musical ensembles that can read rhythms at sight can get immediately to working on the MUSIC rather than wasting precious time being spoon fed individual parts. The key to success with this process is in the planning. Short, sequential rhythm lessons are planned for every class meeting.

THE RHYTHM LEARNING SEQUENCE
Step Five
Understand It

In order for complete mastery to occur, the learners must at some point have a thorough, cognitive *understanding of the theory* of the new rhythm. It should be noted that in the case of very complex new learnings, this theoretical mastery might take a long time to achieve. Small, relevant explanations of theoretical content can be presented again and again in increasingly complex terms until full mastery is attained. In all cases, however, it needs to be remembered that theoretical explanations must always *reflect* the learners' experiences --- never *precede* them.

For ultimate success when using this learning sequence, it is recommended that Steps One through Four follow the regimen outlined so far. Each individual step needs to be the total focus of attention in the precise order presented, and each step must be mastered before advancing to the next. Step Five, however, is very different.

Step Five is important. Before we can say that students have truly mastered a rhythm, we must make certain that they **understand the rhythm** completely. However, we should not wait until Step Four has been completed before we begin helping students to understand the things that they are doing. Explaining and discussing the theory of each new rhythm should occur in *small, relevant doses* throughout the process of learning a rhythm. It can begin as early as Step One. For example, after Mr. Johnston's students had successfully echoed the sound of four sixteenths in 4/4 meter for a couple of days, it would have been appropriate to discuss the fact that these new notes were faster than the students' familiar eighth notes. That small slice of Step Five would probably have been enough information at that time, and it certainly would not have confused the students. At another time, after the students had more experience with the sound and feel of the rhythm, a short discussion might reveal the fact that these new notes are not just "faster" than eighth notes. They are precisely *twice as fast* as eighth notes. This understanding would probably best fit sometime during Step Three, when students could actually see that there are four sixteenth notes on a count, but only two eighths. Still later a more detailed mathematical discussion could occur involving the fact that, because there are four sixteenths on a single count, each individual sixteenth note has to be one-fourth of a count, and so forth.

Step Five's understandings are appropriately sprinkled throughout the entire learning sequence. It becomes our responsibility to know *when to say what* to our students in the effort to get them to cognitively understand what they are already experientially doing. It needs to be stated again at this point that theoretical understandings should never be the focus of attention unless students have successfully experienced the thing that is being discussed. Basically speaking, if students do not understand theoretical content that is being presented, it is probably being presented too soon in the sequence. Students do not yet have enough experience with the rhythm to successfully associate the words being spoken with the sounds being made. When this occurs, the discussion should be immediately dropped and the subject revisited later when the students have more experience with the rhythm.

RHYTHMIC LITERACY

The dictionary defines literacy as the ability to both *read and write* a language. We cannot be certain that our students have achieved literacy in the musical language of rhythm unless we know that they can both read and write rhythms. When our students look at a rhythm and *recite it* (that is, *perform it*) correctly on their instruments, we feel we have succeeded. But the ability to only read a language does not, in and of itself, constitute literacy. Literacy implies a higher standard which, when met, results in even better performance and the ability to work independently to solve problems. A person who does a perfect reading and recitation of the English language sentence, "Their car is one of those fuel-efficient hybrids" would, on the surface, appear to be competent in the English language. However, if that same person consistently wrote that and similar sentences as "There car is one of those fuel-efficient hybrids," we would be forced to admit that the writer does not seem to have as solid a foundation in the language as their reading implied. Although read and recited aloud perfectly, the writing clearly demonstrates a fundamental lack of understanding of the significant differences among the words their, there, and they're. It is important to note that this deficiency is only revealed through the writing of the sentence. An important test for language literacy is seeing how the subject writes the language. That is one of the reasons the English curricula in our schools consist of both reading and writing.

40

For music teachers, a necessary test for rhythmic literacy is seeing how our students write rhythms. Many music students, even those who usually seem to read rhythms adequately, do not truly understand them. They are very often simply following along a millisecond behind a strong reader in their section. The surest and quickest way to individually discover who those students are and to help them achieve rhythmic literacy is through the writing process. Pencil and paper exercises are required in order for students to validate that they have mastered Step Five, *Understand It*. This need not be a time consuming project, and the time that it does take yields significant information relative to each individual student's understanding.

On a certain day, Mr. Johnston has his band students put their instruments away five minutes early. As the students return to the rehearsal room, they are given a half sheet of paper on which they are instructed to quickly compose four measures of rhythm in a given time signature. They are not to have any music books open in front of them. Each measure must contain a different setting of the new rhythm being learned, and the final note in the entire exercise must be a half note. (So that they don't forget this, Mr. Johnston has them write the half note in first). In the example of Mr. Johnston's class as we are currently following it, the time signature would be 4/4, and each measure would have to contain at least one group of four sixteenth notes. After class, very little time is required for Mr. Johnston to determine which of his students need help and which are well on the path toward rhythmic literacy.

by Matthew Dean

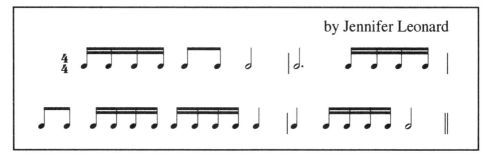

by Jennifer Leonard

Over the course of the next several rehearsals, Mr. Johnston uses the students' individual rhythmic compositions to launch a new series of rhythm exercises for the benefit of the entire group. The students are informed that each time they enter the room, they will see a four-measure rhythm written on the chalkboard. Each day's rhythm will be one of theirs from the quiz, chosen by him to be that day's rhythm warm-up. The rhythms will be written on the board just as they were received. Some days the rhythm chosen will be completely correct, but on other days, the examples will have mistakes in them. Because flawed samples are going to be used, the names of the "composers" will not be written on the chalkboard.

On a certain day, the rhythm chosen is Matthew's from the previous page, one of the ones the teacher found that contained basic errors. Sometime during the group warm-up, Mr. Johnston turns his attention to the chalkboard and asks, "Does anyone see a mistake in today's board rhythm? If you do, you need to identify the mistake and then tell us the absolutely easiest and quickest way to fix it." He asks this same question whether the example on the board is correct or not. Students who are examining rhythms for correctness are bringing into play all of their rhythmic understandings. Today, various students identify each of the writer's mistakes, describing what is wrong and suggesting what they consider to be the best solution for fixing the problem. At times, other students suggest that there might be an even easier way to remedy the situation. This results in a group discussion that has students thinking rhythmically and manipulating rhythms in many, many interesting ways. It is an invaluable exercise which affords the teacher an opportunity to readdress various basic rhythmic fundamentals with the class. And while the class as a whole is reviewing its understanding of rhythm in a general sense, Matthew is receiving the discreet help he needs in a non-threatening, anonymous way. The five minutes of class time spent taking the short quiz in the first place have already paid for themselves many times over.

As each mistake is analyzed and discussed, the teacher corrects the notation on the chalkboard according to the students' wishes, until the class agrees that all four measures are perfect. The exercise ends with the full group counting and then playing the now corrected rhythm on the Bb Scale, one pitch per measure. The students play the first measure all on Concert Bb, the second on C, the third on D, and the fourth on Eb. They then repeat back to the first written measure for F, and they continue on, ending with the last written measure on the octave Bb. And because Mr. Johnston required that the last note in the writing exercise be a half note, the scale exercise ends with a musically satisfying sense of finality.

Rhythmic Dictation

Persons who are judged to be literate in a language also have the ability to transcribe the spoken word into written form. Stated simply, they can write down what they hear someone saying. Persons who are rhythmically literate can do the same thing. They can accurately transcribe rhythmic sounds into musical symbols. This process is usually known in the profession as "rhythmic dictation" and is an exercise that many professionally trained musicians first experience in college. However, it is important to realize that rhythmic dictation is not something that only college-age persons are capable of doing. The very youngest of students can demonstrate great skill in the taking of rhythmic dictation, if they are introduced to the process through a well-planned, sequential program. Such students can certainly be certified as rhythmically literate.

A program of rhythmic dictation needs to be started early in the education of music students. One of the most likely reasons many college music majors experience difficulty with rhythmic dictation is that they are never encouraged to try it until they arrive on campus. Elementary age students should be exposed to the process of writing down sounded rhythms as soon as they are successfully reading rhythms that consist of notes having two different durations. Students who are reading rhythms either on flashcards or in their lesson books that consist of half notes and quarter notes in 2/4, for example, are ready to be introduced to rhythmic dictation. Once again, this does take a small amount of class time, but it yields tremendous rewards.

When introducing rhythmic dictation, it is important that everything possible be done to ensure student success. Students relish the feelings of satisfaction and self-esteem that accompany success. Students who are successful with their first attempts at rhythmic dictation will come to enjoy it. It stands to reason, therefore, that the early attempts at rhythmic dictation should not be graded. Students should feel absolutely no pressure. These first attempts should simply be classroom exercises that are followed immediately by the teacher demonstrating the correct responses on the chalkboard. The first rhythms for dictation should be taken directly from the materials that the students are experiencing in the class. Students should be told the time signature and the number of measures that the rhythm will be before they hear it. The rhythms need to be either sung on a neutral syllable or played on an instrument. The full duration of a half note in 2/4 time must be heard by the students and must resemble the sound of the half notes that they sing or play. The sustained duration inherent in a two-count note cannot be discerned in a clapped rhythm. A clapped half note in 2/4 time sounds much more like a quarter note followed by a quarter rest than it does a half note. The tempo must be given and the example repeated several times.

To help ensure initial success, a "Rhythmic Dictation Shorthand," in which the students basically make a *pictograph* of the rhythm, can be introduced. In this process, students are encouraged to let their pencils "draw a picture of the sounds" first, and then translate their pictures into notation. "Let your pencil play the rhythm on your paper."

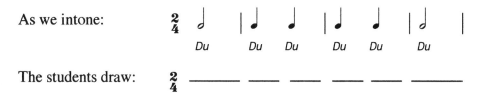

They then demonstrate their understanding of half notes and quarter notes in 2/4 time by putting the correct kinds of notes and the barlines into their line drawing.

This process introduces rhythmic notation in a way that is easy for young students to understand, because it adheres completely to "Foundational Principle No. One." Students have the luxury of first being able to concentrate totally on the rhythm's sound. They simply have their pencils play the rhythm on their paper without their having to think about notation. Then, in a separate act of concentration, they demonstrate their understanding of note proportions by transcribing their dashes into standard notation.

As the students mature musically and begin to have rhythmic dictation examples with "fast notes" in them (sixteenths in 4/4, eighths in 2/2, and so on), the fast notes are drawn close together as dots.

The students record the following "sounds" on their papers:

They then translate their dots and dashes into notation. Over time, students eventually wean themselves from these pictographs and proceed directly to the notation.

Developing students who are skillful at rhythmic dictation is not difficult if it is started early in their educations and if it is done on a fairly regular basis. The most difficult part of this for us is convincing ourselves that we can afford to take the required minutes away from the rehearsal aspects of the class period. This is an important concern, considering that students come to our classes to play or sing. That is why they joined band, orchestra, or choir. We need to plan rhythmic dictation exercises very carefully, so that they take as small a percentage of the class time as possible. An episode of rhythmic dictation can be effectively done in less than five minutes if paper is handed out as students enter the room, and so forth. The rewards of this planning ahead should be apparent. Students who can successfully take rhythmic dictation will not only become excellent rhythm readers, but they will be far more likely to be able to solve their own rhythm problems. Over the years that these students are in their school musical ensembles, this will save untold rehearsal time. Both their present and future teachers will be able to use the four magic words, "Look at the rhythm," and know that the students have been given the tools necessary to solve rhythmic problems on their own. The time spent on rhythmic dictation is an investment that pays for itself many times over.

The Rhythm Learning Sequence in Review

Perform it

Introduce the new rhythmic figure by rote in phrases that are one measure in length. The use of the voice on neutral syllables *(du or tu)* is highly recommended. It is important that the learners be able to concentrate completely on the *sound* and *feel* of the new rhythm. Use the *aural/oral* approach --in the ear and out the mouth. "Listen and repeat after me; my turn, your turn." Students who can vocalize the new rhythm with the proper style and feel have an internalized model of the rhythm being introduced. In instrumental settings, when the learning is transferred to instruments, it is important that the "melody" be so familiar that it requires virtually no thinking -- for example, an already thoroughly well-memorized *Major Scale*. The students need to concentrate just on the sound and feel of the rhythm -- not on fingerings, pitches, or written notation. The full measure of rhythm should be played or sung on each pitch of the scale.

Count it

Upon mastery of Step One, the new rhythm needs to be presented with the teachers' preferred *counting names* ("1-e-&-a" or "Du-ta-de-ta" or "Ti-ri-ti-ri" for example). Do not move ahead to step three in the sequence until students can flawlessly associate the teacher's presentation of the rhythm on neutral syllables with the appropriate counting names, as in the following example: for $\frac{4}{4}$ ♩ ♩ ♫♫ ♩ |

Teacher intones: *Du   Du   Du-du-du-du   Du.*
Students respond: *1   2   3- e- &- a   4.*

See it

With Step Three, it is time to show the learners for the first time *what the new rhythm looks like*. The goal is for the teacher to be able to say to the students, "This is the *look* of that rhythm you *can already do!*" If the sequence has been followed properly to this point, the learners are able to concentrate on only one thing -- what something that they do very well looks like. Measures of rhythm are best displayed on flashcards rather than the chalkboard, and they should initially be played or sung on a single pitch before being performed on a scale, one measure per pitch. Master this flashcard/chalkboard step before moving on.

Test it

If Steps One, Two, and Three in the sequence have been successfully mastered, the learners ought to now be able to *generalize* the rhythm to new situations, such as published etudes or songs which include the rhythmic figure that is being studied. The learners should be able to visually recognize the new rhythm (step 3), call it by name -- in other words, count it (step 2) and perform it in an appropriate musical style (step 1). This fourth step, therefore, serves as an *evaluation tool*, allowing teachers to assess whether or not the learners are able to move from the known to the unknown as independent learners. If not, reteaching of the previous steps is required.

Understand it

In order for complete mastery to occur, the learners must at some point have a thorough, cognitive *understanding of the theory* of the new rhythm. It should be noted that in the case of very complex new learnings, this theoretical mastery might take a long time to achieve. Small, relevant explanations of theoretical content can be presented again and again in increasingly complex terms until full mastery is attained. In all cases, however, it needs to be remembered that theoretical explanations must always *reflect* the learners' experiences --- never *precede* them.

Language Literacy And Rhythmic Literacy: A Comparison

One day in the early 1930's, Shinichi Suzuki, the founder of the world-renowned Suzuki Method of string education in Japan came to an astounding realization. It amazed him that virtually every child in the world easily learns to speak his or her own native language. Not only do very young Japanese children learn to speak Japanese, he thought, but they all learn to speak Japanese in the particular dialects of their various regions. This is obviously not true just of Japanese children. We can all agree that American children born into English speaking families all learn to speak English, but children in Boston, Massachusetts and Mobile, Alabama certainly do not speak the exact *same* English. Hearing children from those two cities say, "Daddy went to park the car," would rather easily identify which child was born and raised in Boston and which in Mobile.

People generally were not impressed with Suzuki's excitement over these thoughts. Many felt that he was being absurd. They generally thought that the ability of children to learn language was a naturally occurring phenomenon. It was an inborn talent, one of the principal ones that separated man from the other animals. Suzuki did not deny this, but he focused his attention on the idea that *it was the method* that was used to develop the ability for language that was resulting in the overwhelming success. He believed that all humans are born with various talents -- language, mathematics, physical movement, music, and so forth, but the degree to which those talents are realized depends upon the methods used to cultivate them. The obvious ability of every normal child to learn to speak their native language at an early age was to him a demonstration of a perfect and amazingly successful educational method. Modeled on the way that children become skillful in language, he named his method for developing children's musical talents "The Mother Tongue Approach." He devoted his life to the idea that this method could serve as the model for developing the inborn musical talents of all children. If children were introduced to music in the same way they were introduced to language, they would be successful.

It is generally agreed that the wonderfully successful "Suzuki Method" cannot be wholly transplanted to our modern system for teaching students in school settings. First of all, Suzuki felt that musical instruction needed to begin at or before birth. School music teachers do not generally meet their students until they are much older. Additionally, the Suzuki method requires an extreme amount of parental involvement, something which is difficult to implement in our fast-paced, modern, western society. These difficulties notwithstanding, it is felt that we can effectively cultivate our students' inborn talents for musical rhythm based on Suzuki's mother tongue approach. Students who are introduced to rhythm in the same way they were introduced to their native language will become "rhythmically talented." The following is an abbreviated summary, showing similarities between the way children become literate in their native languages and in musical rhythm, according to the concepts of our *Rhythm Learning Sequence*.

If the precise order of the five steps of the *Rhythm Learning Sequence* seem at first to be difficult to remember, simply think through the process that we all went through as we became proficient in our native languages. Rhythmic literacy follows the same sequence as language literacy.

Language Literacy

Step 1: Listen and Repeat

Beginning at birth, infants hear literally millions of repetitions of short, meaningful phrases. Early baby babble eventually evolves into understandable individual words. Individual words gradually evolve into two and three word sentences, which the children "perform" over and over again.

Step 2: Associating Verbal Sounds

Not only can the children now clearly say the words "happy" and "sad," but they can correctly associate those words with the feelings of happiness and sadness. The correct name association is verified when the children are asked to put on a "happy face" or a "sad face."

Rhythmic Literacy

Step 1: Listen and Repeat

New music students first hear short rhythmic phrases which are repeated many times. This *"My turn, your turn"* process occurs daily until such time as the rhythms are being performed competently and musically by the new learners. Through imitation, the students learn to "speak" the rhythmic language of their teachers.

Step 2: Associating Rhythmic Sounds

The rhythm learners gradually develop the ability to associate a rhythm sounded on neutral syllables with specific counting names. Students who associate the sound of *"Du Du Du-du Du"* with the words *"1 2 3& 4,"* have made the correct name association.

Step 3: Seeing Known Words in Print

The children who are now verbally confident and fluent are shown simple words in children's books. The first words shown are those that the children have been competently using for a very long time, *"ball, car, mommy, daddy,"* and so forth. The children are concentrating on one thing -- what familiar and well-known words look like in print.

Step 4: Testing Language Reading Ability

Children who can "read" the words *ball, car, mommy, daddy* in their favorite story should be able to recognize and read those words in a new story. If they cannot, their favorite story has simply been memorized. More work is needed on Steps One, Two, and/or Three above.

Step 5: Understanding Language

Before persons can be considered literate in the English language, they must demonstrate that they understand the difference between words like *there, their,* and *they're.* They must study the theory of language known as *grammar.* The ability to only speak and read the language is not enough. Theoretical understanding is most clearly demonstrated through the ability to write the language correctly.

Step 3: Seeing Known Rhythms in Print

Students who can competently perform and count rhythms are shown for the first time what those same rhythms look like in printed form. *"This is the look of that rhythm you can do."* The learners have the luxury of concentrating on only one thing, the "look" of several short, well-known, already musically performed rhythms.

Step 4: Testing Rhythm Reading Ability

The students who can competently "read" rhythms on the chalkboard or on flashcards should now be able to recognize and perform those rhythms in published etudes and/ or literature. If they cannot, more work is needed on Steps One, Two, and/or Three above.

Step 5: Understanding Rhythm

Before students can be considered literate in the language of rhythm, they must be able to demonstrate that they understand the theoretical foundations of the rhythms. The ability to only read and perform rhythms is not enough. A well-grounded, theoretical understanding of rhythm is most clearly demonstrated through the writing process. Students must be able to write rhythms correctly.

The Rhythm Learning Sequence: Conclusions

The majority of us receive little or no preparation for the task of teaching rhythm to students. In college we take courses in harmony, arranging, sight-singing, conducting, music history, and so forth, because they are the foundations of musicianship. Few if any of us are offered a specific course designed to inform us how to teach rhythm. Since all future music teachers have to audition in their applied performance specialties in order to get into music school, it is probably assumed, based on our polished performances, that we are already accomplished rhythmically. There are so many other important things that we need to learn, and there is no way to cram another course into the already overcrowded music education program. Textbooks generally spend little or no time on the subject of how to teach rhythm. Those that do seem mostly to talk about what to do when a rhythm problem arises -- count it, clap it, isolate it, slow it down, and the like. A systematic and well-reasoned approach to the teaching of rhythm can result in a drastic reduction in the number of such problems that occur in the classroom. To repeat a time-honored saying, "An ounce of prevention is worth a pound of cure."

Rhythm reading deficiencies are not confined to students in elementary school, middle school, or high school. The conductor at a well regarded conservatory of music annually complains that, on average, the incoming freshmen simply can't count! He wonders aloud, "What are they teaching in the public schools these days?" Professional conductors who go on tour from city to city and who hire pick up orchestras in each city to accompany their acts report the same problem. Sight-reading problems -- particularly the inability to read rhythms -- become the principal concern of many of these conductors, who have to prepare the ensembles with one rehearsal on the day of the show. Clearly these problems should have been solved long before reaching these adult populations of musicians. In my view, the root of the problem lies in the ways most of us were introduced to the reading of rhythmic notation. We eventually figured it out, but it took much longer than it should have.

Our ability to teach rhythm as a separate and discreet skill is enormously important to the overall success of our music programs. *Things done right the first time* do not require remediation with each new piece of literature. Teachers and conductors do not need to spend precious rehearsal time showing students "how their parts go." Students who are introduced to rhythm reading as the students in Mr. Johnston's class have been develop rhythmic independence and confidence. It is truly a fairly simple process.

The Sequence and the Method Book

The actual teaching of a rhythm using the *Rhythm Learning Sequence* advocated here probably takes no more aggregate time than teaching it any other way, but the results are spectacularly different and long lasting. In actual fact, it may take even less time. Instead of spending all of two 30-minute lessons on a new rhythm, the teacher using the steps of *The Learning Sequence* will spend at the most five minutes per lesson spread out over perhaps ten lessons. That is 50 minutes instead of 60 minutes total time spent on the new rhythm. The problem is that we have to plan ahead in order to know when to introduce Step One, so that by the time our students reach the page on which the rhythm first occurs, they have absolutely no questions about it. In effect, they sight-read the page. All too often, this does not happen. Although the following example is exaggerated, some version of it does occur all too frequently. The teacher is introducing the new rhythm of four sixteenth notes in 4/4 to his class and has not planned ahead. He has laid absolutely no groundwork for what his students are about to encounter as they turn the page in their books.

******

The teacher is finally finished hearing the day's assigned lesson. He notices on the clock that there are only four minutes left, and he must dismiss the class on time. He needs to make an assignment for them to practice for the next class. He asks the students to turn to the next page in their method books, which is the first page in the book that has the rhythmic figure of four sixteenth notes. He proceeds through the five steps of the *Rhythm Learning Sequence* in the following scrambled order, all in four minutes. Keep in mind that the students have no idea what these new notes sound like. They have absolutely no experience playing four notes of equal value spread over one count.

See It. (Step 3)   "**Look**, boys and girls. We have a new rhythm on this page. Do you see the four notes with two beams connecting them in the first measure of No. 1?"

Count It. (Step 2)   "Here is how you **count these new notes**. Can you say this?" *The students echo the teacher's presentation of his* *preferred counting system ("1-e-&-a" or "Du-ta-de-ta" or "Ti-ri-ti-ri," etc).*

Understand It. (Step 5)

The teacher now feels that he has to "teach" the students something about these new notes. "These new notes are called sixteenth notes. They are called sixteenth notes because they are one-half as long as eighth notes. One-half of an eighth is a sixteenth, so they are twice as fast as eighth notes. We know that eighth notes are one-half count each, so if sixteenth notes are twice as fast as eighths, then each sixteenth note will be one-fourth of a count. **Do you understand that?**" *No student really does, but they don't want to be the "dumb kid" in the class, and so no one answers. The students actually have no idea what the teacher is talking about.*

"And if each sixteenth note is one-fourth of a count, then the group of four sixteenths will be equal to one count. 1/4+1/4+1/4+ 1/4 = 4/4, which is the same as 1, right?"

Test It. (Step 4)

The teacher notices that he has only two minutes to get the students out the door, and so he says, "All right. **Let's try No. 1.**" *Not surprisingly, the results are disastrous, and so the teacher says.....*

Perform It. (Step 1)

"No, No. **Listen.** It goes like this. I'll sing it first and then you sing it with me. **My turn, your turn.**" *They do it once, and time is up.* "OK. Your assignment is Numbers 1, 2, and 3 on page 17. See you Thursday."

******

There is very little chance that these students are going to successfully be able to practice this assignment. Sixteenth notes in 4/4 time were presented in four minutes in the sequence of Step 3, Step 2, Step 5, Step 4 and finally, because that didn't work, Step 1. The students were expected to concentrate on everything at once. They had no experience playing the sounds that the teacher was trying to verbally describe, and there was certainly no thought given to mastering anything. Foundational Principles One and Two were both seriously violated. Only those students with someone at home to help them will come back with any idea of what is going on. Some of the students who do practice will be playing the new rhythm incorrectly, which will have to be unlearned at the next class. Most will be frustrated as they attempt to try to understand how a note can be only one-fourth of a count. Young students simply cannot comprehend that. Many will not even try and will adopt the defeatist attitude of "I can't do this. I hate this new rhythm!" If they do practice, they will spend their time just playing something that already sounds good and is satisfying to them. They will *play* their instruments but not *practice* them.

The class on Thursday will not go well, as students have not been able to adequately prepare the lesson. The teacher will be forced, therefore, to spend the entire class period singing to the students to show them how the etudes go. All the while the teacher will be thinking, "I explained all of this to them last class. These kids just don't practice!" Because by the end of the class the students finally seem to be getting the gist of Numbers 1, 2, and 3, the teacher will mistakenly assume that they are now understanding sixteenth notes. However, most of the students are not learning the basics of sixteenth notes. They are simply learning, by way of numerous repetitions, to play Numbers 1, 2, and 3 on page 17 in their books. They will likely need help on the new assignment of Numbers 4, 5, and 6 also, and so the next class will basically be a repetition of this one. And the cycle will continue. Many students will conclude that the way to learn rhythm is by listening to teachers say a bunch of boring stuff they don't really understand, but that eventually the teachers will get around to doing what is required --showing them how it goes! The students are basically being taught by rote, and unless things change, they will have to be shown how to play the majority of their parts, which wastes an immense amount of time over the years. To the students, reading rhythms is confusing, frustrating, and boring, and they need a lot of help with it.

It bears repeating. Teaching rhythm requires planning. *There are some things that we can't afford not to do.* Planning rhythm experiences is one of those things. New rhythms must be introduced by ear, many lessons before students are asked to look at them.

Planning and the Method Book

Modern band, string, and recorder method books provide a basically well-planned-out course of study for young students. They feature instrumental skills that are laid out in an orderly and logical sequence. Generally speaking, Book One in a series introduces one note in the first etude, followed by a second note that is either one pitch higher or lower in a subsequent etude. When these two notes are learned, the next etude features the book's first "melody," a combination of notes one and two, and so on. The books also guide students through a set of rhythms that are introduced one at a time. Each new rhythm is a logical extension of the one just accomplished. Not all books use the exact same starting notes and not all books agree on the same starting rhythms, but all are based upon planned learning activities that are both logical and sequential.

Because the books are so thoroughly and thoughtfully laid out, many of us consider them to be our lesson plans. The books represent precisely what lesson plans ought to be, a step-by-step journey through the necessary skills and knowledge required for the acquisition of the subject matter. As logical as this sounds, there is one serious flaw in it. *Books don't teach; teachers teach!* We would do well to think of our method books as simply logical guides that point out to us a reasonable order in which to introduce the various skills necessary for our students to acquire, but the books don't teach those things. We do.

In a very real sense, method books should be thought of as vehicles that provide convenient and well-written rhythmic materials for us to use as *testing materials*. Our students learn rhythms by mastering the "pre-book" Steps One, Two, and Three of our *Rhythm Learning Sequence*. Students first listen to and repeat rhythms until mastered. Next they associate the learned rhythmic sounds with a particular set of counting words. They then are shown what the rhythmic sounds look like in notation by the use of non-melodic flashcard or chalkboard notation. Not until these three steps have been mastered should method books and melodic notation come into play. Method books basically involve Step Four in the Learning Sequence: *Test It*. Step Four says, "If Steps One, Two, and Three in the sequence have been successfully mastered, the learners ought to now be able to *generalize* the rhythm to new situations, such as *published etudes or songs* which include the rhythmic figure that is being studied. ....This fourth step, therefore, serves as an *evaluation tool*, allowing the teacher to assess whether or not the learners are able to move from the known to the unknown as independent learners."

So far as the teaching of rhythm is concerned, method books serve as *post-tests,* allowing us to assess how effective our teaching of Steps One, Two, and Three has been. I repeat. Books don't teach; teachers teach.

Planning Ahead Made Easy: Marking the Method Book

When teaching rhythm to students using a method book, planning ahead is easier than it might seem. We need simply to go through our *Teachers' Book* at the start of the school term and find each page when a new rhythm first appears. From each of those spots in the book, we need to turn back a few pages and write in the top margin of that page something like, "Introduce *the sound* of sixteenth notes in 4/4 today." Keep in mind that this notation in the margin is several pages in the book before the page that actually contains sixteenth notes. The margin notation needs to be clearly visible, perhaps in colored pencil, so that we see it immediately upon opening the book to the current lesson. During the warm-up that day then, we first introduce the sound and feel of sixteenth notes. Step One in the Learning Sequence has been initiated, several lessons before these new notes will be seen by the students. On the next page, the notation written clearly in the margin might say," Continue Step One; sixteenths." Perhaps the next page will say, "Introduce *the counting* for sixteenth notes." On one of the next pages, "Show sixteenths, Use flashcards." On one of the pages right before the page which actually introduces students to sixteenths, the margin notation might say," Short *rhythmic dictation*; sixteenth notes." By simply implementing our own margin notations that have clearly outlined the first three steps of the *Rhythm Learning Sequence*, we have solved the planning ahead problem. We have given our students the necessary background needed in order for them to be able to successfully sight-read the first sixteenth notes in their books.

The margin notations at first ought to be written in pencil, as it may take a couple of times through the book before we figure out how much time is enough lead time for the various rhythms covered by the book. If not enough time is at first allocated and the students reach the new page before they have mastered Step Three of the new rhythm, it would be far better to review something or do any other meaningful activity rather than press ahead in the book. It is tremendously important that our students find nothing rhythmically on the new page that they have not already done. When we determine that either too little or too much time was allotted for a certain rhythm, the margin notations need to be erased and adjusted either forward or backward for the benefit of the next class to go through the book.

There will be occasions when students are working on two different rhythms at the same time. For example, they might be finishing up their work on sixteenth notes with flashcards just before actually seeing them for the first time in their books, while at the same time listening to and repeating the next new rhythm in the book. This creates no problems for students. They are not being asked to concentrate on more than one thing at a time. With the first rhythm they are concentrating on *seeing* a full measure of music containing a now familiar rhythm at a single glance, and with the other they are simply being introduced to *a new sound*. This situation, as a matter of fact, adds a refreshing bit of variety to the class. Student concentration is enhanced when classes consist of a series of mini-lessons within the timeframe of the class period.

Beginning Lessons

Ideally, effective rhythm education will begin in the first year of instruction. It is imperative that our students develop a healthy attitude about rhythm early. Once they develop a negative attitude about rhythm, it is difficult, although not impossible, to get the situation turned around. The way that beginning lessons are formatted has much to do with the acquisition of a success-oriented attitude about rhythm. Once again, planning is the key. The four-minute, unplanned introduction to four sixteenth notes described earlier must be avoided at all costs.

It is not possible in this book to lay out the perfect lesson scenario, since there are so many variations of schedules in existence. In addition to class lessons, there are private one-on-one lessons. Class lessons throughout the world are grouped as either homogeneous or heterogeneous. Meetings last 15 minutes, 20 minutes, 30 minutes, 45 minutes, once a week, twice a week, everyday, during the school day, after school, and on and on. Recorder lessons are frequently just a portion of the general music class period. No matter these differences, however, a general framework for any and all lessons can be laid out that will help all of our students to be successful rhythmically.

To be the most successful, teachers need to have *one overriding goal* in mind for every class and student that is taught. This goal is so important that all others pale by comparison. Stated as succinctly as possible, we need to say to ourselves at the start of every lesson:

56

> "It is my responsibility to make certain that these students leave today's session with all of the skills and knowledge they need in order to successfully prepare the lesson that I am going to assign."

We need to check the time throughout the lesson to make sure that the students understand and can perform the material that is going to be assigned for them to work on at home. In short, we need to *teach to the assignment.*

We learn whatever we practice. There is nothing in the human brain that protects us from learning material that is being practiced incorrectly. The incorrect reading of a rhythm that is being practiced at home by our students is being imprinted on the brain in the exact form that it is being practiced. Lessons in which the majority of teacher time is spent fixing mistakes that the students "mastered" at home are neither productive nor are they positive experiences for students. The students feel that they have failed. Unfortunately, poorly prepared lessons start a vicious cycle. Because the students were not adequately prepared for the assignment that was given at the last lesson, the majority of time in the current lesson is spent trying to help them with their old assignment. This in turn results in another last minute assignment, and on and on and on! This cycle must and can be broken.

Format for a 30-Minute Instrumental Class

A suggested plan of time management follows, modeled on a 30-minute, instrumental class lesson. Depending upon the objective for any particular class meeting, adjustments in the minutes allotted for each segment will need to be made, but the *meat* of the lesson — the middle — will, generally speaking, receive the greatest percentage of the class time. Students must have the tools necessary to successfully practice the assignment if the next lesson is to be successful.

First Eight Minutes (approximately 27% of total class time)
Students enter the room which, if possible, has been set up beforehand with the correct number of chairs, stands, and so forth. In beginning string classes, the instruments have been pre-tuned if possible.

Individual Warm-up

Students begin to warm up individually. This assumes that students have been taught *how* to warm up and *why* it is so important. This warm-up procedure needs to be constantly monitored. It must always be considered by students to be a serious activity. During this period, much individual attention can be given by teachers as they circulate around the room. Practice records can be checked. Pats on the back can be awarded for good posture. Hand positions, bowing, embouchures and so forth can be individually corrected. Individual student questions can be answered.

Group Warm-up

The automatic warm-up is strongly recommended (see page 16). With no fingerings or notation to think about, students can be encouraged to concentrate on posture, hand position, bow arms, breathing, tone quality, intonation, and so forth.

Daily Rhythm Lesson.

Steps One, Two, or Three of the *Rhythm Learning Sequence* to one or more rhythms. Flashcard or board rhythm emphasis on any rhythm that will be included on the assignment that is going to be made at the end of the class is highly recommended.

Middle Fifteen Minutes (approximately 50% of total class time)

Begin the *lesson part* of the class with the playing of a familiar, good sounding review song or etude. This should be something the teacher is virtually certain that the students can play without difficulty.

Hear the day's assigned lesson (three to five minutes)

If the students were properly prepared for success at the last lesson, the assigned lesson will proceed smoothly and will take a small amount of time. If the quality is not acceptable, analyze the reason and take remedial action. If it is necessary to repeat part of the assignment, try to make the repetition varied. Perhaps have the students memorize one of the etudes to be repeated. Not only is this something that is probably not done on a regular basis, but it almost certainly will require that students practice! At any rate, memorization is a valuable musical skill for students to acquire. It allows them to concentrate on the sounds they are making, not on the ink blots they are seeing.

Teach to the new assignment (ten to twelve minutes)
This is the most important part of the class. The students must leave the room with all of the tools they need to be successful if they practice. If the assignment is the first time the students are seeing a new concept in the book, it might be a good idea to actually have them "group-learn" the first etude of the assignment during class. This will likely ensure that their home practice session gets off to a correct start. The etudes that follow that one should not be gone over in class, however. Students need to experience the pleasure that comes from working it out for themselves.

Last Seven Minutes. (approximately 23% of total class time)
First *close* and then *end* the class. (approximately five minutes)
Bring *closure* to the class by having various students discuss or demonstrate what was learned during the class. Students verbalizing what was learned helps them to cement the learning into long term memory. It also helps the students to realize that they actually are learning. Progress on an instrument is slow and steady, and students sometimes do not realize how much they are learning.

End the class by having everyone play something that is satisfying and sounds good. Try to always end the class by making music.

Final Two Minutes.
Remind the students of their assignment and dismiss them on time, so that they are not late getting back to their regular classroom or to their next class. This dismissal procedure must always include time to properly care for instruments — loosening bows, wiping rosin, swabbing woodwinds, emptying condensation, closing brass tuning slides, covering percussion equipment, and so forth. Students will learn to care for their instruments if they follow the above procedures at the end of every class under our guidance.

Teaching Rhythm in Performing Ensembles

Students in ensembles that do not regularly use a method book should still be introduced to new rhythms using the *Rhythm Learning Sequence*. In those cases, planning ahead is just as important and is also quite easy. Before handing out any piece of literature that we want to use, we should first go through the score and take note of the various rhythmic figures that we find.

When we see one that we are not sure that our students can play, we need to test the students. Sometime during a warm-up period, the rhythm in question needs to be included in a board rhythm or on flashcards. If the rhythm is successfully played, the students are ready to sight-read the piece. If, on the other hand, the students cannot perform the rhythm and they seem confused about it, then *that piece of literature should stay on our desks*. It should not be handed out. In those situations we need to begin with Step One of the rhythm in question and proceed through the sequence until we feel certain that the students have mastered it. It does not matter how long that may take. It will save time in the long run. Older students can generally proceed through the sequence more quickly than younger ones, especially in cases when the unfamiliar rhythm is simply a slight variation of a basic rhythm that was previously mastered. When the piece is finally handed out, our students should see absolutely nothing that is fundamentally new to them. Our question, "Does anyone see a rhythm anywhere in this piece that they don't under-stand?" should bring no responses.

The key to rhythmic success when using literature lies in not putting any piece of music in the students' hands if it contains basic rhythmic concepts that they have not mastered. *In sight-reading, students should encounter only new settings of familiar rhythms*. This results in rehearsals that are de-void of constant stops to teach parts. The rehearsals are more musical and certainly more enjoyable for both teachers and students.

Can Rhythm Be Learned Through Literature?

The advertisement in the music journal really entices us. One of our favorite composers has just written a new piece described as "... a great piece for teaching 6/8." We know that our students ought to experience at least one piece this year that is written in 6/8, but we also know that putting off doing a piece in 6/8 is really easy to do. It seems like such a struggle to get the students to understand and to accept 6/8. We can get them to under-stand that eighth notes get one count, because they have already been taught the definition of the bottom number of the time signature. But we also know that the composition in question is actually in compound 6/8, meaning that eighth notes are really one-third of a count. The piece will not sound musical until and unless it is done "in 2." What is the best way to get from one concept of eighth notes to the other? Should we start the piece out in a mod-erately fast six and gradually shift into two, asking the students to feel the big beat only on counts one and four? Or should we try to introduce it in two beats to the measure right from day one? Perhaps this piece is going to have the answers to these questions. After all, the advertisement does say that this is a great piece for teaching 6/8.

The piece is bought, handed out, learned with difficulty, and eventually successfully performed. After the concert, we feel really good about the whole process. We have gotten the 6/8 monkey off our backs. Our students have learned compound 6/8! Now that they have accomplished that, we are free to do another piece in 6/8. It is during the sight-reading of this second piece that cold, hard, depressing reality sets in. The students can't begin to sight-read it. They are obviously not able to generalize the 6/8 rhythms that they "learned" in the first piece to the rhythms they see in this one. We are ultimately forced to recognize that they didn't actually learn 6/8 in any kind of a general sense. They simply learned their individual parts to that one specific piece of music. In our minds we were teaching 6/8. In their minds they were learning their parts, the sounds required of them to make that one particular piece sound good. Unfortunately, the new piece is going to have to be taught the same way the first one was, with myriad stops to teach small groups of students how it goes while the other students sit and listen.

Rehearsals like these actually can cause irreparable harm to a piece of music. The music is dissected into so many little pieces and parts that it is, in effect, butchered. Because each rehearsal seems to be a process of pounding notes into students' heads, the musical message of the piece becomes obliterated. Our students actually end up hating the piece of music, because "getting it" was such an unpleasant struggle. Even after a successful performance of the piece, students will actually say, "I hate that piece. We had to practice it every single day forever!" In these situations, nothing is gained, and something is probably lost. Lost is any hope of getting our students to willingly embrace the next piece in 6/8.

No piece of literature ever written can teach students 6/8, or any other meter for that matter. No composer writes a piece of music in which the first few measures of the piece introduces everyone to the easiest rhythm in that meter, followed by everyone having the next logical rhythmic figure for the next few measures, and so forth. Composers have no interest in sequencing everyone through a succession of rhythms arranged from the simplest to the most complex. Their emphasis is in writing *music*, not in writing *music lessons*. In order to make a musical statement, composers obviously have different parts performing different rhythms at the same time throughout the piece. Giving 100% of the students the luxury of concentrating on one thing at a time by giving them all the same rhythms simultaneously throughout the piece is simply not possible if meaningful music is to be created.

The solution to the problem is fairly simple and is repeated here for emphasis. *The piece should not have been handed out.* While the music still sat on our desks, 6/8 should have been introduced to the students according to the *Rhythm Learning Sequence.* When all of the students were successfully taking rhythmic dictation in 6/8 , reading 6/8 etudes in two beats to the measure without difficulty, and so forth, then and only then, should the piece have been issued to the students. When asked, "Does anyone see a rhythm that they don't understand?," there would have been no responses, and the students would have sight-read the rhythms in the piece. When and if rhythmic problems arose, they would have been quickly fixed, most likely by the students themselves. The second rehearsal of the piece could have gotten right to the expressive qualities of the composition. In addition, pieces two and three in 6/8 could be sight-read as well. Once 6/8 is learned independent of literature, it can be applied to all 6/8 literature. We repeat: Contrary to what the advertisements suggest, *no piece of literature can teach rhythm.* That is not the purpose of musical literature. We must teach the rhythm and then give our students the opportunity to implement it in the literature.

The above is not to be confused with concert pieces that are correlated to specific pages in the method books of various publishers. Such concert pieces do not profess to teach rhythm. In fact, they implement rhythmic elements exactly as they ought to be. The pieces are designed to be studied only after the students have successfully completed the units in the method books that cover the performance skills needed for a musical performance of each piece. These correlated pieces allow students to experience how their learned skills of rhythm, articulation, dynamics, style and the like, combine to make "real" music. The learned skills are brought to the literature, not the other way around. Teachers who use these products simply need to make certain that the students have truly accomplished the skills presented in the method books before handing out the concert music. If the method book etudes have basically been learned in class by rote and have not been individually mastered and understood, there will be abundant trouble with the correlated concert pieces as well.

The Process of Music Education in Performance Groups

The foregoing discussion concerning whether rhythm can be learned through literature or whether it should be learned first and then brought to the literature represents two different philosophical views of music education in performance groups. The question to be answered is this: What is it that we should be doing on a daily basis to help our students achieve an education in music? It all comes down to a question of *ends and means*. We can all agree that the end goal is musically educated students, but what is the means we employ to achieve that goal?

One school of thought says that the means we use to reach the goal of producing musically educated students is *musical literature*. A person who ascribes to this philosophy, when asked about the process of music education, would answer something like this:

> It is a process of exposing students to good musical literature that is written at increasingly more difficult and complex levels as they mature in their musicianship. As they proceed from performing simple arrangements in elementary school to doing more advanced literature in high school, they become accomplished performers and, therefore, are musically educated.

Proponents of this model believe that as students study various pieces, they acquire a diverse set of performance skills, the accumulation of which ultimately results in their being musically educated. By learning "Piece A," they learn to perform in 6/8 and they learn to do a fortepiano. "Piece B" teaches them syncopation and staccato articulation. Through "Piece C" they learn to sing or play expressively in a legato, sustained style. As a result of their working on and eventually performing "Piece D," they not only come to understand cut time, but they learn to play triplets as well.

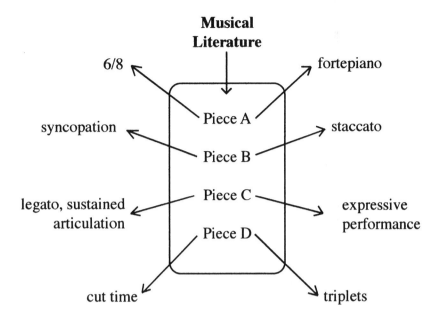

Those who follow this model obviously believe that pieces of music serve as the central means for educating their students. Musical literature is the engine that drives the machine toward the end goal of producing skilled performers. They tend to search the literature to discover which exact performance skills the students will learn as they study each piece. Directors who bought the "... great piece for teaching 6/8" described before would definitely believe in this model of music education in performance groups.

Another teacher, when asked the same question, would say something quite different:

> It is a process of teaching 100% of the students a series of basic musical skills, which are logically arranged from the simple to the complex and which are then applied to the body of appropriately graded literature for the purpose of aesthetic pleasure.

Those who follow this model believe that the central means for educating their students lies in the acquisition of a set of basic performance skills. *Only after a skill is mastered* is it implemented in appropriately graded literature, allowing students to successfully put the acquired skill to use in musically expressive performances. The already accomplished skills are brought to the literature. **Mastered skills** are the means by which the literature is experienced.

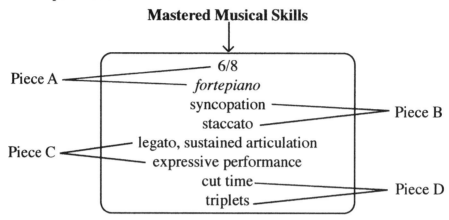

It should not surprise anyone that we wholeheartedly endorse the second of these curriculum models. What we ought to be doing on a daily basis in our classrooms is teaching musical and technical skills as the means to experiencing and enjoying the body of musical literature. Experience has shown time and again that reversing the process does not work very well. Literature can not and should not be used as a means to achieve performance skills. Performance skills are the means by which the aesthetic impact of the literature is experienced. Mastered skills come first; then the literature.

The Two-Part Rehearsal:
The *Lesson* and the *Literature*

Since rhythm cannot be effectively learned through literature, it is essential that rhythm study be allotted its own segment of the rehearsal. Our students need to concentrate on rhythm as a separate entity in order to gain the skills, knowledge, and confidence necessary to independently and successfully apply their rhythmic abilities to the literature. As Lowell Mason declared in the 1830's, "... to teach but one thing at a time -- rhythm, melody and expression to be taught and studied separately, before the child is called to the difficult task of attending to all at once." A short, logically sequenced, well-planned rhythm lesson needs to occur every day that the class meets. It is important that this rhythmic component utilize the automatic warm-up concept referred to earlier for the first three steps of *The Learning Sequence*. 100% of the students must be involved in the lesson and have the luxury of concentrating on nothing else. To be most effective, the rhythm lessons and the literature being studied by the group should be dynamically linked. Students need to experience applying their already learned rhythms to the literature in order to bring true relevance to the learning process. If our students spend a considerable amount of time learning to perform and to understand quarter note triplets in 4/4, for example, then that rhythmic figure ought to be in a piece that we hand out once the rhythm is mastered. Students will be more inclined to take their daily rhythm lessons seriously when they realize that the things they are learning pay off.

The Lesson Segment:
The Group Private Lesson

If music education in performance groups is indeed "... a process of teaching 100% of the students a series of basic musical skills, which are logically arranged from the simple to the complex ...," then there needs to be time set aside every day for that exclusive purpose. The first part of every rehearsal, therefore, becomes **The Lesson Segment**. This part of the rehearsal might well be thought of as a *group private lesson,* a time when 100% of the students are taught those concepts and skills that they all need to know and be able to do in order to successfully experience the literature. The daily rhythm study is but one of many such important lessons that occur during this part of every class period. Other basic procedures and skills as well need to be introduced, isolated, studied, practiced, and mastered by all of the students before the literature is encountered in the rehearsal. A representative few of these many lessons are listed below:

1) The standard for posture must be taught during this segment of the rehearsal and reinforced daily throughout the entire school year.

2) Wind and choir students need to understand that posture is critical to breathing, which in turn is critical to excellent tone production. You can't have one without the other.

3) All students need to be taught how to warm up and why warming up, both mentally and physically, is essential to excellent performance.

4) Students need to understand that excellent tone production is directly linked to intonation. You can't tune a bad tone that is producing few overtones.

5) Intonation needs to be studied and learned as a separate discipline before it can be effectively worked on in the literature. All students need to be able to talk knowledgably about the scientific bases of intonation. They need to understand sound waves that are out of phase and the resulting beats of poor intonation. They need to develop the performance skills required to eliminate beats as they tune to others. Winds need to know the general tuning tendencies of their instruments and how to adjust individual pitches.

6) Students need to understand that the most important interval to be tuned is the octave and that they need to listen to the lowest voices first and match the overtones that those lowest voices are setting in motion.

7) Through the studying of chorale-type literature during the lesson segment of the rehearsal, students must experience the sound of chords that are beautifully in tune, giving them a model of the sound they are trying to achieve as they work on vertical intonation in the literature.

8) 100% of the instrumental students in the ensemble need to master the various styles of articulation that will be encountered in the literature.

9) All instrumental students need to be able to play the scales associated with the pieces in the folder. They should also be able to write the key signatures of the scales they play.

10) And, of course, it is during this part of the rehearsal that students must be guided through the steps of the *Rhythm Learning Sequence*. "A rhythm a day..."

The Literature Segment:
The Literature is Experienced

After each day's group lesson is completed, the literature is rehearsed for the remainder of the class period. If the daily lessons that start each class meeting have been carefully and thoughtfully planned, the students will not be confronted with any basic skill that is foreign to them in the second part of the class period. During the group lessons, the students have been given the time needed to master those basic skills required in order to have a successful and pleasurable encounter with each piece under study. Obviously, there will be mistakes made during the rehearsal of the literature, but the students will most likely be able to understand and address the mistakes in an efficient way, based on the firm foundation they have achieved. A hypothetical *one-way bridge* connects the two sections of the class period.

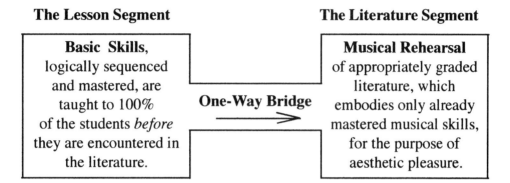

The Lesson Segment		**The Literature Segment**
Basic Skills, logically sequenced and mastered, are taught to 100% of the students *before* they are encountered in the literature.	**One-Way Bridge** →	**Musical Rehearsal** of appropriately graded literature, which embodies only already mastered musical skills, for the purpose of aesthetic pleasure.

The One-Way Bridge

The accumulated mastered skills of the first part of every rehearsal are carried into the literature segment. It is during this second part of the class period that students need to have a meaningful, aesthetic interaction with the music. The only goal in this part of the rehearsal is to involve students in the emotional experience of making music. All students deserve to make beautiful music everyday. Students who are touched aesthetically every time they are in band, orchestra, or choir will, in large part, sign up for the class year after year. The single, most important aspect of retaining students *in* music involves getting them hooked *on* MUSIC.

In order to maintain the artistic integrity of the literature segment of the class, it is important that we make no attempt to cross back over the one-way bridge and interrupt the musical flow of the rehearsal. Obviously, problems with tuning and intonation, balance and blend, appropriate style, articulations and so forth, will need attention, but these must not be new, basic skills that are unknown to the students. They are already-learned skills that now need to be applied to this particular piece of literature. With the mere mention of the word "staccato," for example, all of the students will know precisely what the director feels is deficient. There will be no need to stop the music making to teach the students how to perform in a staccato style.

There will be times during the rehearsing of a piece of literature that a basic skill will be found that needs to be taught or, at the very least, reviewed. Our students will occasionally struggle, for instance, with a rhythm

68

that it was assumed had been previously mastered. If after a couple of quick attempts to help them with it, they are still unsure of the rhythm, the remediation needs to be ended for that day. Being aware of the fact that this part of the class is for making music, we should simply make a mental note of the deficient skill and move on to another section of the piece or change to the next piece. Obviously the rhythm in question needs to be taught or reviewed, but not now! It needs to become the focus of attention beginning with the lesson segment of the next rehearsal. Further, the particular problem spot in the piece should be avoided in subsequent rehearsals until 100% of the students have mastered the problematic basic skill. *There should be no teaching of basic skills during the literature segment of the class period.* There should be only the application of already-learned skills.

This is a difficult thing for many of us to do. It is something we have to work at until it starts to feel right. We have been trained to find and fix errors that are standing in the way of fine performance. That is what we do, and it is a concept that is obviously valid and should not be compromised. The question is *when* the required remediation should take place. Let's imagine a band rehearsal in which a rhythm problem occurs involving quarter note triplets in 4/4 time. It is a rhythmic figure that we mistakenly assumed was part of the group's rhythmic repertoire. The figure occurs only one time in the piece and in only one instrumental part. Those of us who follow our instincts and stop to correct this oversight immediately will be working with a very small number of students while the others sit doing nothing. It will not be a quick fix, as this is not a rhythm that can be taught in a couple of minutes. Unfortunately, the aesthetic momentum of making music has been stopped, while the majority of students sit and listen to a few of their classmates get a lesson.

The folly of this situation is that the students getting help with quarter note triplets in 4/4 are probably not learning the fundamental structure of that rhythmic figure anyway. They are simply learning, by rote repetition, one particular measure in one particular piece. Additionally, the next time the ensemble has a piece with the same rhythmic figure, it will likely not be the same students who have it. We will once again have to stop the music to teach a new group of students the same rhythm. And the beat goes on. Every time we encounter quarter note triplets in 4/4 time, the music making will have to come to a halt while a few students are taught their parts. Clearly, every student in the class needs to be able to recognize, perform, and understand this rhythmic figure. The few minutes spent teaching it to all of the students during several lesson segments over a period of time will, in the long run, save a great deal of time and frustration on the part of everyone.

Teaching During the Literature Segment

Teaching obviously occurs during the literature segment of every class meeting, but the teaching is not of basic, fundamental skills. The important teaching that takes place during the second part of the rehearsal involves those things that bring the literature being rehearsed to life:

-- how the form chosen by the composer is important to the musical performance of the work,
-- how the composer's life experiences might have affected the thematic materials,
-- a discussion of why the trombone theme seems so angry sounding compared to what everyone else has,
-- how the style of the writing compliments the lyrics of the poem,
-- why the composer might have chosen the title that he or she did,
-- why the composer wanted this section of the piece to be so much softer,
-- which of the group's various styles of articulation best conveys the composer's intentions for this particular section of the piece, and so forth.

During the last part of every rehearsal, the literature is taught. Students experience how skillful composers combine discrete musical skills to create meaningful music. Our band, orchestra, and choir classes become *MUSIC* classes, in the finest sense of that word.

All of our rehearsals must end with students making music. More than anything else, that will bring them back next time, ready and anxious to be in the class for another day.

The Four Magic Words:
An Assessment Tool for the Teacher

If the group private lessons of the first part of every rehearsal have been effective, sentences of approximately four words in length can *magically* result in significant and meaningful change during the second part of the class period when the literature is being explored. When a rhythm problem occurs in a piece, for example, we ought to be able to stop the group and utter these four words, "Look at the rhythm." The students should have the ability to fix the problem themselves, because they have been given the time necessary to master the rhythmic concepts in question during the daily rhythm lessons. If the students are playing or singing too loudly and we say, "Look at the dynamics," the dynamics should be adjusted immediately without further time-consuming words from the podium. If the piece is being performed in an inappropriate style, the four words, "Think about the style," should result in an immediate change to a more suitable style. "Look at the articulation" or "Think about your diction" should solve any problems in those areas. "Look at the key" ought to remedy key signature problems, and on and on.

Obviously, the four magic words do not work unless those concepts and skills have been mastered by the full ensemble during the lesson segments. If *"Look at the _____"* does not result in positive change, then we can safely assess that the concept or skill in question is not part of the students' repertoire of mastered skills. Teaching or review is required during the next and subsequent lesson segments, but never during the literature segments. In the two-part rehearsal format, basic musical skills are taught to 100% of the students in the first part of the class period, and music is made in the second part.

Percentage of Time Devoted to Each Segment of the Rehearsal

What percentage of a class period should be devoted to the lesson segment, and what percentage to the literature segment? There are probably as many answers to that question as there are musical groups. Every situation is different. At the start of a new school year, a middle school/junior high school ensemble might spend 80% of its class time establishing a firm skill basis, leaving only 20% of the time for rehearsing the literature. If the literature has been carefully chosen to match perfectly with the mastered skills, however, it will be a musically satisfying way to end each class. Even though it is only 20% of the total class time, it is *quality time*. The school year will be off to a musical start. As the year goes forward, the percentages ought to gradually shift to 70/30 -- 60/40 -- 50/50 -- 40/60, and so forth to the end of the year, when the percentage might be 10/90. This division of time is something that we must constantly monitor. If our students are frequently struggling with the literature, a couple of things may need adjustment. Perhaps a greater percentage of the class time needs to be spent building a firmer skill foundation, or the chosen literature does not accurately reflect the basic skills that the students have mastered.

Significant Advantages of the Two-Part Rehearsal Format

Our students learn best by making music. They are happiest when they are playing or singing. The more they participate in these activities, the more they learn and improve and the more pleasure they derive from being in the class. Students who are in bands and orchestras and choirs that adhere to the principles of the two-part rehearsal format play or sing a great deal more than do other students. During the lesson segment, 100% of them are actively involved and learning for the vast majority of that time slot. When they cross over into the literature segment, all of the students are also participating for a much greater percentage of that time period as well, since there are no long stops for teaching a few students a basic skill. It stands to reason that students who play or sing under the guidance of a skilled teacher a great deal more than other students will improve their performance proportionally. The more our students make music, the more they improve. Musicians learn by doing more than by any other means.

When the two-part rehearsal format is working as it should, the literature is experienced as MUSIC from the very first encounter. The literature is not cut up into little bits and pieces because the students can't figure out their individual parts on their own. With as few as four words, we can get our students making music again. The emphasis is on the music, not on the notes. That, of course, is how it ought to be.

Finally, the two-part rehearsal format can go a long way toward alleviating discipline problems in our rehearsals. First of all, students who are playing or singing are not doing other things. It is very difficult to play the clarinet and talk at the same time, although some especially ingenious students have probably figured out how to do that! However, students who are learning and who are involved in making beautiful music actually have no interest in disrupting the process. It is the farthest thing from their minds. Students are much more likely to willingly follow the behavior guidelines of the class, because they genuinely want to make music. We do not need to become policepersons. Music itself becomes the disciplining force in the classroom.

A Comparison of Elementary and Secondary Planning

As discussed earlier, planning for success in the elementary instrumental program is mostly contingent upon our knowing precisely what will be assigned for home practice at the end of each class, and then teaching to that assignment. This guiding principle was stated this way: "It is my responsibility to make certain that these students leave today's session with all of the skills and knowledge they need in order to successfully prepare the lesson that I am going to assign." The most significant part of each class period in the elementary program is spent teaching those basic skills that the students will need in order to return to the next class with the assigned material well in hand.

In a very real sense, planning for success in the secondary performance program is the same, but with a shorter time frame. The guiding principle for the secondary director can accurately be expressed as follows:

> "It is my responsibility to make certain that these students leave today's lesson segment with all of the skills and knowledge they will need in order to have a successful and musically satisfying encounter with the literature that is going to be rehearsed in the second part of the class period."

In both of these cases, the process involves giving students the tools they need in order to do the assigned job. A group of trade school students should not be sent out to build a house if those who will be the carpenters have no skills with a hammer. Shortly after they start to frame the house, all work on the structure will have to be stopped. The student electricians, plumbers, and others will be forced to sit with nothing to do, because they can't play their parts in the process until the framing is up. All of the bent nails will have to be pulled, and the student carpenters will need to be given lessons on how to use a hammer. They will need to be shown where to grip the handle for maximum force at the head, the importance of the wrist, and so forth. These lessons will then need to be followed with a sufficient amount of practice in the art of hammering. Not until they can efficiently and accurately drive nails into practice pieces of wood can work on the house resume.

On the other hand, had the hammering lessons preceded the actual start of the house, the student carpenters could have immediately enjoyed seeing how quickly the walls went up. Instead of the incredible embarrassment of knowing that everyone else was sitting around waiting for them to get their part right, they would have been able to feel great pride and personal satisfaction at how well they nailed the framing together. They could have gained insight into the important function that their contribution plays in the finished product. They could have begun to imagine what the completed structure might look like.

We in music must not send our students out into the musical literature without the tools they need in order to be successful. Certainly one of the most basic, all-encompassing, and important of those tools is the ability to independently read and understand rhythms. Rhythm is the framework upon which the notes are hung. Unless that framework is established first, student musical ensembles will encounter significant frustration and disappointment with all of their musical endeavors. Countless students will be unable to contribute their parts to the project until others have received remedial help with their particular assignments in the overall structure. It is our responsibility to equip our students with the rhythmic skills and understandings they will need in order to have a meaningful and satisfying experience making music.

Part Two

An Expanded Discussion of Step Five: *Understand It*

A New Look
at an
Old System

I am convinced that there are two major problems with the way we teach rhythm to our students. The first of these has been examined thoroughly in Part One of this text. In order to be successful, music teachers need to introduce the process of rhythmic literacy to their students in a definite, understandable, and logical sequence. Teachers need to plan ahead in order to launch each particular rhythm's sequence well before the students will see that rhythm on the printed page. Five sequential steps have been laid out and carefully illustrated to help students achieve rhythmic literacy. The last of the five steps, labeled **Understand It**, is perhaps the most troublesome of all, however. Our own understanding of the structure of rhythmic notation and the ideas that we pass on to our students as a result of those understandings, comprise the second major problem with rhythm education. *Much of what we tell our students as we endeavor to get them to understand rhythm doesn't really make much sense.* We try to convince our students that rhythm is simple and logical, but much of what we are telling them is based on illogical assumptions. It is little wonder that they don't understand it. This illogical foundation has been passed down through the generations of musicians for centuries. It would behoove all of us to step back and take a fresh, new look at the system of rhythmic notation from its very beginnings. All of us need to be challenged to question our own personal understanding of rhythm. As was stated in the introduction to this book, this examination will absolutely require an open mind. A blank rhythmic slate upon which new and seemingly controversial ideas can be written could very well result in dramatic changes in the way our students understand rhythm. Part Two of this text deals exclusively with Step Five of the Rhythm Learning Sequence; **"Understand It."**

****

A Self-Test

PLEASE DO NOT TURN THE PAGE until you have complied with the following simple request. It will take you no more than a few seconds to complete, and the results will be referred to consistently throughout this part of the book.

Please sing, either aloud or to yourself, the following:

> A one octave major scale, up and down in quarter notes.
> Do not repeat the top note. Set your own tempo.

Your Test Results

I call the preceding exercise a test, because I feel that it tests our core understanding of the system of rhythmic notation. Grading each of your tests is, of course, an impossibility for me. There is obviously no realistic way that I can know what each of you actually sang. However, I am willing to wager that, in fact, I do know. Over the years, I have done this same exercise with countless college methods classes, entire music faculties of various school systems, individual music teachers, college professors, composers, conductors, skilled amateur musicians, and so forth. The results have always been the same. They have never varied. My instructions are similar to those on the preceding page, except that with a group, I must give a starting pitch, tell them what "words" to sing, and I must set the tempo.

> "Good morning, ladies and gentlemen. Please sing this pitch with me. Thank you. Using that as your starting pitch, I'd like you to sing me a one octave major scale, up and down in quarter notes. Let's use solfege syllables, and we'll not repeat the top note."

> I then begin to snap my fingers at a comfortable tempo and, as I continue snapping the tempo, I give the instructions a second time:

> "You're going to sing a major scale from this pitch, one octave up and down in quarter notes, using solfege. Do not repeat the top note. Ready, sing........"

I have always gotten the exact same response -- a one octave major scale up and down, with each note being sung for one count at my prescribed tempo. That, of course, does not seem at all surprising. As a matter of fact, the initial thought is that the "test grade" should certainly be an "A." However, I then begin to ask a number of questions, which at first hearing seem to border on the ridiculous.

1)   "Let me ask you something. *Why did you sing each pitch for one count?*" I immediately notice a sea of frowns, confused expressions, and silence, which I interpret as their wondering why I would ask

such a silly question. Someone in the group finally offers the obvious answer, "because that's what you asked us to do." We then review my instructions, and everyone agrees that I actually asked for a major scale "in quarter notes." I did not ask them to sing one count notes; I asked them to sing quarter notes. Without thinking, they had equated my term *quarter notes* with *one-count notes*. I immediately caution them not to dismiss this as something frivolous until they hear me out, and I then proceed to ask them to consider a whole string of new questions.

2) "Have any of you ever done a piece of music in which the quarter notes received a half-count?" Everyone agrees that, taken as a group, they have literally done millions of half-count quarter notes. It is most often called cut time or alla breve.

3) "Have you ever done a piece of music in simple 6/8 in which the eighth notes get one count? How long are those quarter notes?"
   "Two counts," comes the response.

4) "Have you ever done a 6/8 march? How long are the quarter notes?"
   "2/3 of a count."

5) "When working out a difficult sixteenth note passage, have you ever asked your students to give each sixteenth note one count, so that the concentration could be on fingerings or pitches? In that moment, how long are quarter notes?"
   "Four counts."

6) "In working out a really difficult thirty-second note passage on your own applied instrument, have you ever given each thirty-second note one count so you could concentrate on fingerings? If so, theoretically how long are the quarter notes?"
   "Eight counts."

7) "Have you ever done quarter note triplets in 4/4 time? How long is each quarter note in the triplet figure?"
   "2/3 of a count."

8) "Have you ever done quarter note triplets in cut time? How long is each quarter note in that triplet?"
   "1/3 of a count."

It cannot be denied that almost every accomplished musician has done eight-count quarter notes, four-count quarter notes, two-count quarter notes, one-count quarter notes, two-third count quarter notes, half-count quarter notes, and one-third count quarter notes. Yet when asked to sing a scale in quarter notes, without questioning or discussion, the quarter notes have been one count. Overwhelmingly, we seem to automatically associate the term "quarter note" with "one count." However, when challenged to stop and think about it, we have to agree that quarter notes actually have many durations. *Quarter notes are not one count!*

At this point, it is tempting to dismiss this entire discussion as something not very important. Quarter notes have different durations in different meter signatures. Everyone knows that. We start with the assumed value of the one-count quarter note, but when performing music in certain other meters, we simply have to make adjustments to the durations. In cut time the quarter notes are "cut in half." In simple 6/8 the quarter notes are "twice as long." It's really not that difficult to figure out, and so this discussion is basically just a matter of splitting hairs. It is not something worth getting upset about, and there is certainly no need to overhaul the basic way we think about rhythmic notation.

A Significant Problem

There is one terribly important and significant problem with this argument. Admittedly it is rather easy for mature, already-trained musicians to make the above note value adjustments and calculations when required, ***but it is extremely difficult for young people to understand!*** The vast majority of students are introduced to the task of reading rhythmic notation long before they are developmentally able to think abstractly. They think largely in concrete terms, and once they learn that quarter notes are one count, they fervently resist any other interpretation of the quarter note. Experience has shown time and time again that they just don't get it. To illustrate the difficulty involved in getting young people to understand and accept the fact that a single note symbol can represent multiple durations, let's take an extended and detailed look at how we teach and how students learn cut time.

Cut time
(Alla Breve -- 2/2)

We are going to focus on cut time, because it is something that all young musicians must learn to do. Students don't like it and most teachers would rather avoid having to teach it, but it has to be done. Much choir literature is written in cut time. Every beginning band and orchestra method has a section devoted to the teaching and learning of cut time. However, since it seems to be rather difficult to comprehend, in most published method books it is not introduced until Book Two. Unfortunately, this is actually part of the problem. Cut time is not introduced until the students have spent a great deal of time performing only one-count quarter notes. They have concluded on their own that the musical symbol known as the quarter note is music's icon for the number "1." This becomes so thoroughly established in their concrete-thinking brains that they energetically resist anyone who tries to tinker with that "truth."

Many sources can be found offering advice on how to introduce cut time to our students. Text books, journal articles, music bulletin boards, and so forth can be accessed for help with this subject that seems to be a difficult one for students to grasp. Many of these sources seem to conclude that understanding and accepting cut time is something that just takes time. Eventually the students will "get it," just as we did. The following are some examples of the various ways we approach the teaching and learning of cut time.

My own first experience with cut time is something that I will never forget. I was one of three or four students in a pullout instrumental program in a very small public elementary school in Pennsylvania. I was personally having a very difficult time learning to read music, because I had been playing the trumpet by ear since the age of four. I found it to be extremely boring to be practicing whole notes followed by whole rests, when I had the ability to play far more challenging and interesting things by ear. I would spend perhaps two minutes working out of the beginning method book that my Dad bought me, and then spend the next half-hour or so just playing for fun. But I persevered and was finally getting this music reading idea. One day our teacher brought to our little band class a piece of music to learn that was written in cut time. His explanation of cut time really confused me. I had worked so hard learning that whole notes are four counts, half notes are two counts, and quarter notes are one count. Now I was supposed to change all that and give all the notes half as much? I was not happy about this turn of events, and so I did something about the situation.

When I got home that day, I took a pencil and I put a stem on all of the printed whole notes. Next I filled in all of the printed half notes, and finally I beamed together each pair of quarter notes. In other words, I physically changed the notation to 2/4, and then I read the piece like a champ. At the next class, I was the only one who had any idea of what was going on. I remember to this day my sense of pride as the teacher praised my comprehension of the new time signature. But my feeling of accomplishment was rather short lived, because the teacher walked behind me midway through the lesson and saw what I had done. He saw that I was not understanding cut time at all. I was simply reading 2/4. The sad conclusion to this story is that the teacher thought what I had done was a really good idea, and the other students' assignment for that day was to go home and do the same. That's how we learned cut time.

A few years ago I placed one of the college's student teachers with a terrific middle school band director in the area. I scheduled my first supervisory visit for the end of the student's first week of practice teaching. It was understood that she was certainly not ready to do a full rehearsal, and so I would observe her as she simply warmed the group up. What I was not prepared for was how tremendously short the warm-up would be. One time up and down the Concert Bb Scale, one time through a short unison etude, and she was beside me asking if we should go somewhere quiet for our post-conference. I explained to her that I had just gotten started with the necessary paperwork that accompanies all observations. I suggested that she just wander through the band as her cooperating teacher worked with the students, and I would signal her when I was ready.

The band's regular teacher took the podium and said something that immediately made me stop my paperwork. After announcing the piece the students should get up, he said, "Now remember. This piece is in cut time, *so all of the quarter notes are eighth notes.*" I was sitting off to the side of the ensemble where I could see the faces of many of the students. I looked at them to see how they reacted to such a pronouncement. They showed no expression whatsoever as their teacher magically changed quarter notes into eighth notes. I, on the other hand, was dumbfounded. It occurred to me that this excellent band director at one time or another must have said to himself, "All right. We'll give the quarter notes a half count if the composer insists, but they're NOT going to be quarter notes! They are eighth notes!"

As I was driving home, I was reliving this experience in my mind. I fantasized that those same 8th grade band students moved as a group the next period to their Visual Arts class. Just before turning the students loose on their new project, I imagined the art teacher saying, "Now remember. These are no longer oil paints, they are watercolors. So red is blue, blue is yellow, and yellow is green." Can you imagine the uproar in the class? "Mrs. Cole, you can't change the basic colors! How are we supposed to remember what's what?" The art teacher calmly responds, "Wait just a minute. Last period you didn't object at all when the band director changed music's basic notes. He changed whole notes to half notes, half notes to quarter notes, and quarter notes to eighth notes just because your new "project" was in a different *meter.* When we change *media* here in my class, why can't I change art's basic colors -- red to blue, blue to yellow, and yellow to green? It's the same thing."

It is easy for us to see how ludicrous it would be if the art world changed the names of the basic colors as they switched from oil paints to watercolors. The exact same color would be called red in an oil painting and blue in a watercolor. Obviously, red has to stay red, no matter the media. In music, quarter notes have to stay quarter notes, no matter the meter. To do otherwise invites chaos. As a young boy, in order to hold on to my unshakable belief in the one-count quarter note, I changed my quarter notes into eighth notes by physically joining each pair of quarters together with a beam. Many years later I found an excellent band director who was basically asking his students to do the same type of thing. He did not ask them to take pencils and physically change the quarter notes into eighth notes, but he did ask them to mentally perform the same task. They were to *look* at quarter notes but *see* eighth notes. "Now remember. This piece is in cut time, so all of the quarter notes are eighth notes." He had probably discovered, through experience, that his students were so absolutely certain that quarter notes are one count that they simply found the concept of cut time easier to understand if they changed note *names* rather than change note *values*. In their minds quarters always have to get one count, and eighths always have to get half of a count. So, if the notes in a certain composition are to receive one-half of a count, then they have to be eighth notes. They still look like quarter notes on the paper, but they're really eighth notes now. Confusing for young students? You bet. Wrong? You bet.

Many other instrumental teachers use a less radical approach to introduce cut time to their students. They first ask them to turn back in their lesson books to a group of easy 4/4 etudes and songs. These are review materials that the students encountered a long time ago, and they can play them easily now that they are more advanced on their instruments. The obvious advantage of this method is that the students can focus fully on this new idea of cut time, because the notes and fingerings are already learned. The teachers usually begin by having the students review the first etude as written. Then they ask the students to play it again, but in a faster 4/4, followed by a third time in a very, very fast 4/4. The students, who have been tapping their feet during these renditions of the etude, are asked by the teachers if their feet are getting tired and, of course, the answer is *"yes!"*

The teachers then reveal their method for introducing the students to cut time. They do them a "favor" by having them play the etude again, still at the very fast tempo, but with one change. To save wear and tear on their tired foot tapping mechanisms, they are instructed to tap their feet only on counts one and three, which the students are more than happy to do. This results in what is actually a pretty interesting phenomenon. The students are doing the musical equivalent of rubbing their stomachs and patting their heads. Their feet are in cut time, but their heads are in 4/4.

This bimodal approach to cut time continues until the students demonstrate that they are comfortable playing in a fast four while tapping in the more leisurely two. At this point the teachers put the finishing touches on their method. The students are to continue calling the first count in the measure "one," but they are to call the third count "two," and call the second and fourth counts "&." Their old *1-2-3-4* becomes *1-&-2-&*, and that's cut time. And we wonder why students are confused. They will do it, but most young students will not truly understand how "3" can become "2." From personal experience I know that some students never advance beyond this concept of cut time. A principal-chair college instrumentalist in one of my Methods classes explained to us one day that half notes are actually still two counts in cut time. You just tap once for the two-count note. In other words, half notes are two *counts* but only one *beat*. He could not come up with an answer, however, when we asked him how he would teach his young students the meaning of the bottom number in the meter signature of 2/2. His students' lesson books are going to inform them that the bottom number of the time signature indicates the kind of note that receives one count. So their books will be telling his students that the half notes receive one count, but he will be telling them that the half notes receive two counts. It seemed to us a very confusing idea for his future students to grasp. Of course, he can come up with some sort of an explanation, but not one that the majority of his students are likely to understand. They will say they understand it, but they probably won't.

Finally, many teachers approach the teaching of cut time from a purely intellectual perspective. First of all, they teach the students that the cut time sign (¢) is another way of writing 2/2. Then they make certain that the students understand the traditional meaning of the bottom number in time signatures. Because this particular time signature tells them that half notes are one count, all of the other notes will also have to change value. Proportionally, whole notes must be twice as long as half notes, quarter notes half as long as half notes, and so on. The teaching is basically a math lesson, which is followed immediately by the students working their way through the cut time unit in the method book. The problem with this very rational and technically correct approach has been alluded to before. Because all of the half notes that the students have played up to this point have been two counts, they are convinced that the two-count half note is the *one and only true half note.* The idea of a one-count half note is just "not right." Those who say that cut time is something that just takes time for students to become accustomed to are correct in that assessment. They will eventually get it, but it won't come any easier to them than it came to most of us.

These and other methods that we use to teach cut time all eventually work, at least to the point that the students are able to play their parts in the cut time literature that their ensembles perform. The sad truth, however, is that most of them have most likely just learned their individual parts to that particular piece. Their sight-reading of the next cut time piece shows very little, if any, improvement. Very few students seem to say, "Oh, good! Another piece in cut time." That is why many ensembles routinely sight-read cut time literature in a fast 4/4 and only later switch to two beats to a measure. Cut time is still a highly confusing time signature for most students. No matter the approach used, countless students still ask this very interesting and challenging question: "Mrs. Brown, if the people who wrote this music wanted a two-count note, why didn't they just write a two-count note?" Obviously they are referring to the half note. This self-learned, fully ingrained belief by students that each of music's note symbols represents an unchangeable rhythmic value is the principle reason that students have difficulty accepting any music in which the bottom number of the time signature is not a four.

As they mature, most students seem to become no fonder of cut time. I laid out the following hypothetical scenario to countless college students over the years: "It is the first week of school and you are auditioning for your chair in the school's major performing ensemble. You have practiced diligently all summer, and you are confident that you are performing better than you ever have in your life. After listening to your prepared pieces, the conductor indicates that he is extremely pleased with your work. His demeanor lets you know that you will be seated very high within your section. The last thing he needs to have you do is sight-read a demanding etude that he has personally composed in order to make certain that no one has ever seen it before. He informs you that he has prepared two versions of the exact same etude. One version is written in 2/4 and the other is in cut time. Understanding that your chair in the ensemble depends heavily upon the quality of your sight-reading, which version of the etude would you choose to read?"

Over the years, I never had a single student indicate that they would choose the cut time version.

The Good News!

> The good news is that none of this confusion and discontent over cut time is necessary. Cut time can be taught in 30 seconds with 100% comprehension and acceptance by students as young as 4th grade --- GUARANTEED! All that is required is some *outside the box* kind of thinking by teachers.

Quarter Notes Are Not One Count

We unwittingly allow our students to believe that music's notational symbols represent specific numbers. *This is the single, biggest detriment to their understanding of the system of rhythmic notation.* Our students are convinced that the musical symbol known as the whole note represents the number "4." The half note stands for the number "2." The quarter note is music's way of saying to young students, "Play or sing me for one count." We do not actually tell them these things, but that is what they experience, and the things that students experience impact them in a much more profound way than do the things they are told. These experiences begin at a very young age. Elementary teachers hold up a card with quarter notes on it, and the class recites *"Ta, Ta, Ta, Ta"* or a similar vocalization that is clearly a series of one-count sounds. Often the card has no meter signature on it, just a picture of four quarter notes. A half note is *"Ta-a,"* clearly a two-count sound. After four or five years of that kind of general music experience with rhythmic notation, the students who go into instrumental music purchase their first method books. All of the quarter notes will be one count in the overwhelming majority of those first books. The students will use the books for perhaps a year or more. By the time they first encounter cut time in Book Two, they have been literally brainwashed into believing that note symbols represent specific, concrete numbers. It is absolutely no wonder that they have difficulty accepting cut time. Their question, "If the people who wrote this music wanted a two-count note, why didn't they just write a two-count note?" makes perfect sense. It is based on their many years of experience with music reading.

Gerald Eskelin, the founder and conductor of the L.A. Jazz Choir, wrote a delightful and enlightening book entitled, *Lies My Music Teacher Told Me.* The book is dedicated to "... all those who studied music just long enough to be thoroughly confused."

Lie #13: "A quarter note gets one beat."

(Stage 3 Publishing, Woodland Hills, CA; 1994, page 117).

Where does this faulty kind of thinking come from? Unfortunately for our students, it comes mostly from us. Intellectually we know that quarter notes are not one count, but when we hear the term quarter note, our gut reaction is one count. Think back to the self-test we took a few pages back. If you did not sing one-count notes when the test asked you to sing quarter notes, you are a rare individual, at least as far as my experience goes. Ask all of your musician friends to sing you a scale in quarter notes and see what happens. No matter what we tell our students when we are teaching cut time or any other meter in which the quarter note is not one count, we totally destroy the legitimacy of that information by what we have our students do. "Let's warm up this morning to the C Major Scale in quarter notes." The students play each note of the scale for one count. Without realizing it, we have just revealed to our students that we truly believe that quarter notes really are, by default, one count. It matters very little what else we may say about quarter notes when we are trying to teach cut time or simple 6/8, and so forth. As we have stated before, students learn *what they do* much more profoundly than they learn *what we tell them*. As a matter of fact, if what we tell them contradicts what we are having them do, they seem to be programmed to dismiss what they are hearing. They will invariably favor what they have done over what they have heard. The learning is in the doing.

Countless published materials help to perpetuate the idea that note symbols have default numerical values attached to them. On the first pages of beginning instructional music books, the "Fundamentals" of music are often introduced. Students are shown the musical staff, the clefs, barlines, measures, and so forth. The books also introduce the students to the musical notes. Pictured first is usually a whole note with the definition that "whole notes receive four counts." Other books more correctly expand upon the above definition, saying that "whole notes receive four counts in 4/4 time." Of course, since this is the students' first music instruction book, they most likely don't understand time signatures. The time signature information on the page tells them that a quarter note receives one count before they have any experience with quarter notes. The quarter notes in the book are several pages away. This is all very confusing to the new musicians and so they just dismiss it, but one thing doesn't confuse them. The open, oval-shaped note is called *a whole note* and it *gets four counts*. Amid the information overload of the "Fundamentals" page, that is something they can memorize. Whole notes are four counts!

Some modern method books include a glossary of terms in the back of the book. The glossary either augments or replaces the beginning "Fundamentals" pages. Book Two of a well-known instrumental method has a glossary entry in the "W's" for "Whole Note." It says, very simply, that whole notes equal four counts. That is not at all unusual, except that this particular book contains an entire unit on cut time! What are the students to think? Their academic teachers have taught them that the ultimate authority for the meaning of a word is the dictionary. The "dictionary" in the back of their music book states that whole notes are four counts, but in the current unit they are struggling with, whole notes are two counts. It is no wonder that they don't consider cut time to be a legitimate time signature. To them, cut time is the illegitimate offspring of 4/4, the "right" time signature.

And what about us? How did we acquire this idea that note symbols carry with them default numerical values? From our teachers, who got it from their teachers, who got it from their teachers, and on and on. Because it has traveled down through the centuries does not make it true, however.

When we are forced to think about it, we have to admit that quarter notes are not one count. Yet when we are asked to do something "in quarter notes," without thinking we respond with one-count sounds. This leads inexorably to only one possible conclusion. Whether we have ever given it any conscious thought or not, we basically believe that rhythmic notation is based on the principle of 4/4 time. It is the genesis of the system. That is why, when we tell our students to do a scale "in whole notes," everyone understands that we want each scale degree to receive four counts. There is no need to mention the time signature. 4/4 is music's default time signature. It is the standard by which all other time signatures are measured. They are like 4/4, but with certain differences. In 2/4 there are only half as many counts in a measure. In 2/2 all of the notes are half as much. In simple 6/8 all the notes are twice as much, and so on.

In many people's minds, there is clear justification for the idea that 4/4 is the founding principle of the system of rhythmic notation. The alternative way to indicate that a piece is in 4/4 is to use the meter signature that we refer to as "common time." It is indicated by something that resembles an uppercase letter C at the beginning of the piece. This would seem to support the idea that 4/4 is rhythm's "Common denominator." A little research into the history of musical notation reveals this to be an incorrect assumption.

In the years between 1150 and 1450, Gothic monks developed a highly sophisticated system of rhythmic notation. Being devout and pious Christians, they defined music with a metrical pattern of three as "perfect time" --- three, as in the Father, the Son, and the Holy Spirit. Music in three was labelled *tempus perfectum.* To denote that a piece was to have a metrical pattern of *tempus perfectum,* they decided upon what they considered to be nature's most perfect geometrical shape, the perfect circle. When performers saw the metrical sign O, they knew that the musical pulses, based on the text, were to be grouped into threes. Music in four did not, of course, relate to the Trinity. It was defined as *tempus imperfectum.* Quite logically, it was decided that if the perfect circle was to represent tempus *perfectum,* then the geometric shape to represent tempus *imperfectum,* music in four, would not be a perfect circle, but rather a broken circle, C. Over time this imperfect circle morphed into something resembling the English capital letter **C**, and the English language name "Common time" somehow became attached to it. It was never intended that this symbol represent the idea that 4/4 was the common foundation upon which the system of rhythmic notation was built. The ℃ symbol was originally meant to represent what was essentially considered a more or less second class, imperfect meter.

The Founding Principle of Rhythmic Notation

4/4 is not music's default time signature and, therefore, the whole note is not automatically four counts. If the whole note does not equal four, what is it's value? The answer is disarmingly simple.

$$
\begin{aligned}
\mathbf{o} &= \text{x} \\
\text{𝅗𝅥} &= 1/2 \text{ x} \\
\text{♩} &= 1/4 \text{ x} \\
\text{♪} &= 1/8 \text{ x} \\
\text{𝅘𝅥𝅯} &= 1/16 \text{ x}
\end{aligned}
$$

The founding principle of rhythmic notation is *a simple algebra formula*. Yes, it could very well be that $x = 4$ more often than it equals any other number, but it cannot be denied that there are literally billions of pieces of music in which the whole note *(x)* equals 2, and 8, and 16, and even 32 and 1. Somehow over the centuries, musicians have taken one single solution to the formula, the $x = 4$ solution, and basically said that this one solution to the formula is the formula itself! From a math science point of view, this makes no sense. Mathematical solutions are the result of mathematical calculations which are based on underlying mathematical formulas. By their very nature, math formulas result in a variety of outcomes, depending upon the values inserted into them. Music's math is based on the above formula, not on just one solution to that formula. In algebra, *x* does not represent a single, unchangeable number. In music, *x* is not exclusively 4. That is what our students need to learn, and the earlier they learn it, the better.

It took me many, many years to come to the realization that our system of rhythmic notation is basically a simple algebra formula. To me it had always seemed logical that the basis of the system was 4/4 time. In fact, it seemed so reasonable that I could not understand why my students could not comprehend and accept meters in which the quarter note was not one count. All they needed to do was make some rather simple adjustments to the well-learned, tried and true 4/4. In retrospect I realize that my students were unwittingly trying to alert me to the fact that something was wrong. What was wrong was my own understanding of the system of rhythmic notation. I was trying to convince my students that the system was logical and made a great deal of sense, but it turns out my understanding of the system was based on an illogical premise. The note values associated with the time signature of 2/2 are not the result of a comparison to the note values associated with 4/4. They are completely independent of 4/4. They are simply the result of a different value for *x*.

The note values in 2/2 result from the fact that in 2/2:

$$x \ (\mathbf{o}) = 2$$
$$1/2 \ x \ (\text{♩}) = 1$$
$$1/4 \ x \ (\text{♩}) = 1/2$$
$$1/8 \ x \ (\text{♪}) = 1/4$$
$$1/16 \ x \ (\text{♬}) = 1/8$$

Teaching Music's Algebra to Students

Unfortunately, these revelations, exciting as they were to me, left me with an even bigger problem. I realized that early in their music studies, our students need to know that music's *x*, the whole note, is not a static number. From its very inception, music's whole note was designed to have changeable durations. It is an indisputable fact that whenever whole notes change value, all the other notes, by their very nature, must also change. The durational values of all of music's notes are derived from the way they relate to the whole note, not from the way they relate to 4/4 time. The only thing that we can say about the value of the half note that will be true in every instance is that it is one-half the value of the whole note. *The whole note is the key that unlocks the mystery.* Our students need to know that changeable whole notes are the norm, not the exception. But how could I possibly go about teaching young students to understand the underlying algebraic foundation of rhythmic notation? I had struggled in vain for years simply trying to get them to understand how note values in other meters relate to those in 4/4. Would they be able to understand these new, even more abstract ideas?

After a long internal struggle with these questions, I must admit that I basically just gave up. I realized that I personally did not have the ability required to structure musical algebra lessons that would be meaningful and understandable and interesting to young thinkers. And I knew that they had to be interesting. Bored learners don't learn! It was clear to me that my students' minds were not yet developmentally ready to comprehend the abstract ideas inherent in algebra. I reluctantly agreed with many others that the students would *someday* be mature enough to figure it all out. In the meantime, my job was to simply expose them to various meters. Given time, they would eventually get it, just like I did.

But then something wonderful happened. I awoke one morning, and the answer simply came to me. Suddenly everything seemed so very clear and simple and straightforward. I felt that I finally really did get it! I had already correctly admitted to myself that I couldn't *explain* rhythmic algebra to my students, but I could certainly get them to *do* rhythmic algebra. Basically, I needed to follow the advice of my own *Rhythm Learning Sequence* --- the experience before the explanation. This new perspective on rhythmic notation needed to be presented as *living* music theory, not as *lectured* music theory. I realized that we can introduce our students to music's algebra without ever uttering the word "algebra." Students can begin by *experiencing* music's algebra, without explanation.

******

It is the spring of the year, and the first-year band class is well beyond the "beginner" stage. The group warm-up is the five-note automatic warm-up (Concert F down to Bb) as described on page 17.

Teacher:	Good Morning. We're going to play our five-note warm-up this morning to whole notes. *A whole note, without time signature, is drawn on the chalkboard.*
	Before we do that, though, I have a question. Let's see how wide awake Amanda is this morning. Amanda, what is today's date?
Amanda:	It's April the 7th.
Teacher:	Correct! Class, in honor of today, this morning's whole notes are going to be seven counts.
Several Students:	Whole notes can't be seven counts! You can't do that!
Teacher:	Yes I **can** do that *(said playfully)*. When our classroom door is open, the principal is the boss around here, but when it's closed like it is now, I'm the boss, and don't you forget it! And in honor of today, the boss says that whole notes are seven counts. Instruments up. Ready, play. *The students dutifully play seven-count whole notes down their five-note warm-up. At the start of each new pitch, the whole note on the chalkboard is pointed to by the teacher.*
Teacher:	Good job. And now I'm going to ask the hardest question I will probably ask anyone all day. Who's up to the challenge? Christopher?
	Christopher, if today is the seventh -- think carefully now -- what was yesterday's date? *(Lots of chuckling in the class).*
Christopher:	*(As though deep in thought)* Uhm. Was it the 6th???

Teacher: Right! Class, because we did not meet yesterday, we
                   need to also honor yesterday, right? Whole notes are
                   six counts. Ready, play. *The class plays the warm-up
                   again, now giving each whole note six counts.*

                        ******

Nothing more is said about what has just taken place, and the class moves
on to other lesson activities. There is little doubt, however, that many students are wondering about these strange and different warm-up activities,
and that is a good thing. Students who are curious are trying to figure things
out. Wondering is a creative and imaginative way of thinking.

The next few times the class meets, the same warm-up routine is followed. A whole note is drawn on the board, and its value announced. "Whole
notes are three; Ready, play." "Whole notes are one." "Whole notes are four."
(It is important that students know that whole notes can still be four counts,
just not all the time). The students especially enjoy it when they are instructed
to give the whole notes one-half of a count each --- the first note on the
downbeat and the next on the upbeat. Their innate sense of musical phrasing, however, makes them want to play the final whole note longer than a
half-count. Their teacher doesn't allow it. *All* whole notes, including the last
one, must be one-half count. No *fermata* allowed. The last note is short.

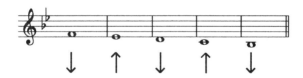

And on the days the class does "Whole notes are two," the students are
obviously playing in cut time. They don't know it, and the teacher doesn't
tell them. The students are not confused. They are not concerned. They have
no questions. They are simply playing two-count whole notes, one of many
whole note values they have recently experienced. They are playing in cut
time without a word of explanation. Could there possibly be a better way for
students to experience the concept of cut time for the first time?

These variable-count whole note warm-ups continue until such time as
the teacher writes a whole note on the chalkboard and the students answer
the question, "How long are whole notes?" with responses like, "as long as
you say," or "any number of counts." At that point, the teacher knows that
the students have a basic understanding of the fact that in music's algebra,

the whole note *x* is a variable. They cannot begin to explain it in "algebra-speak." They know it not in words, but in deeds. They have established the experiential foundation necessary for understanding it when the time for explanations arrives. They are well on their way to knowing the basic structure of rhythmic notation.

Variable-Count Whole Note Melodies

These chalkboard, variable-value whole note warm-ups need to be followed by written melodic etudes and songs that reinforce the idea that whole notes were intended to have variable values. All of the whole notes the students have ever played from written notation have been four counts, and so that is what they have learned and locked into their memories. The students need to experience playing written sheet music in which the whole notes are not four counts. They need to read some melodic materials in which the whole notes are admittedly rather bizarre -- seven counts, five counts, one-half-of-a-count, and so forth. Because they are playing them, they will remember them. Just talking about them will not work. They need to experience them. Some have said that experience is not the best teacher; it is the *only* teacher. After playing melodic materials with the above kinds of values, the students certainly won't think that there is anything odd about playing melodies with two-count whole notes. Their experiences with wildly variable whole note values, simply stated, are an effort to "de-program" them. Whole notes are not four counts!

Teachers can start out by having students go back and play the etudes on the first pages of most beginning method books but, unfortunately, there are very few of them in most books. To extend the experience, teachers are encouraged to make worksheets like the sample that follows. The melodic materials used in the worksheets should purposely be extremely simple. The students deserve the luxury of thinking about the various values of the whole notes rather than about fingerings, and so forth. Perhaps surprisingly, some students will experience difficulty performing an etude like the first one on the worksheet, because they have never before seen a seven count measure. The students are encouraged to hear a small inner voice singing the words *"1-2-3-4-5-6-7"* as they play each note. Additionally, they are encouraged to visualize the numbers flash before their eyes as they play the exercise. Students who both *hear* the inner voice and *see* the numbers will perform the etude flawlessly. An abbreviated, sample worksheet follows.

There are two important things to know about whole notes.

- They are *always* called whole notes. That will *never* change. √ No matter how many counts they get, the name stays the same.

- Whole notes can receive *any number of counts.*

Although you are probably most familiar with four-count whole notes, much music is written in which whole notes do not get four counts. To introduce you to this kind of music, we are going to have some fun. In the exercises that follow, look inside the big whole note to see how many counts to give the notes in each exercise.

4 **Twinkle, Twinkle Little Star**   Wolfgang Amadeus Mozart

Other worksheets that the teacher makes for the students introduce them to whole rests. The students are told that, because they have the same name, *whole notes* and the *whole rests* receive the same number of counts. If the whole notes receive three counts in a certain etude, the whole rests in that same etude are also three counts. To the students this seems simple and logical, and it makes sense to them. Same name, same counts.

As they progress through worksheets like the sample one printed here, the students actually perform in cut time whenever they play etudes like the third one, in which the whole notes are two counts. Cut time is not discussed; it is just played. Students best learn what we tell them when *the telling reflects and follows the experience.* Cut time can be explained later. For now, students just need to be doing some two-count whole notes.

It is important that students play from written notation that features variable-count whole notes consistently over a period of time. At the most, two or three minutes a day at every lesson should be spent on the worksheets. Admittedly, the worksheets are technically easy enough that they could easily be played in one class period, but their impact would be minimized if that were to occur. Students need to experience over and over that whole notes can have variable values. They have known only four-count whole notes for a number of years. The knowledge that whole notes also have other durations cannot be internalized in one class period.

These kinds of worksheets allow the students to *experience through performance* whole notes that have many different values, many of them admittedly bizarre. This purposeful use of highly unusual whole note durations has somewhat of a *shock value* on students and helps them to forever remember that music's whole note does not exclusively represent the number four. The occasional student who may ask, "Can whole notes really be seven counts?" can be told that they definitely do exist, but most likely only on these worksheets. If no student brings it up, it is probably best left unsaid. Music students need to start *thinking outside the 4/4 box* inside which they have unwittingly become trapped. Playing seven count whole notes will help to open their minds to the fact that note symbols do not have default durational values attached to them. Until that lesson is learned, accepting cut time and *all other meters in which the quarter note does not get the beat* becomes a protracted and unnecessary struggle.

Half Notes

Once the teacher feels certain that the students have a functional understanding of whole notes in musical notation, he begins what may well be the most important lesson of all, **the half note lesson**. The goal now is for students to understand that everything about half notes is logical and simple and makes sense. Students begin to develop a good attitude about rhythm, because they start to realize that they can easily figure things out for themselves. They don't need their teacher's help. It is here, with the half note, that they begin their individual journeys toward rhythmic independence.

******

Teacher:	Good Morning. We're going to play our warm-up this morning to six-count whole notes. *A whole note, without time signature, is drawn on the chalkboard. The warm-up is played, one time, flawlessly.*
Teacher:	Good job. Now watch carefully what I do. *He walks to the chalkboard and adds a stem to the whole note.* Tell me. What have I done to the whole note?
Max:	You put a stem on it.
James:	You changed it into a half note.
Teacher:	Correct. But you know what? I've often wondered why it's called a half note. It seems to me that I could remember the name better if it was called a "stem note." Why do you suppose somebody gave it the name "half note?"
Leah:	Because it's half as long as a whole note?
Teacher:	Right, Leah. Did everyone hear that? Say it again, Leah.
Leah:	Because it gets half as many counts as a whole note.

Teacher:	Class, I'm going to test you to see if you've been listening and thinking. Absolutely no talking. Do not help your neighbor. Everyone needs to do their own work. We are going to play our warm-up again, but this time to half notes. *He points to the half note on the chalkboard.*

We will play one half note on each pitch of our warm-up, but I need to tell you something. *Whole notes are still six counts!* This is a test to see if you really understand what a half note is. Remember, you are going to play half notes. Whole notes are six. Think about what Leah told you. Instruments up; Ready, play.

The students play the warm-up, giving each half note three counts. The teacher is obviously delighted. He realizes that these young people have a comprehensive, theoretical understanding of half-note-ness.

******

The students are introduced to the theoretical function of half notes by being shown that the symbol of the half note is directly descended from the whole note. A half note is described as *a whole note with a stem added.* In other words, there is a *visual relationship* between the note symbols, which is one of the reasons he often refers to all of the notes as a *"Family of Notes."* (Younger students might enjoy the notion that whole notes and half notes both have the same oval-shaped face). Secondly, the students discover that the name "half note" was extremely well chosen and is completely logical. Half notes receive one-half the number of counts that whole notes receive. There is a *mathematical relationship* between the notes. These two relationship ideas, visual and mathematical, set the pattern that will be used throughout the year to introduce quarter, eighth, and sixteenth notes to the students. They will come to know that rhythmic symbols and their resultant durations form a highly logical and sequential construct that is easy to understand.

But by far the most important learning that students take from the study of the half note is the idea that *it is their job to figure out how long half notes are!* The teacher never tells them how long they are. The duration of half notes is not a fact to be memorized, but is instead something that the students are expected to calculate on their own. It is their job, not their teacher's. The only math skill required is the ability to calculate the fraction one-half, which is traditionally the first fraction that students ever encounter in their lives -- "you may have half a cookie." For many years students have dealt with the concept of one-half of something and, because they have experienced it, they understand it very well. For them the calculation is extremely simple, and they are very good at it. This, then, becomes the foundation of a healthy student attitude about rhythm. Such students, when encountering rhythmic difficulties later on in their musical studies, will be much more inclined to think, "Let's see, I can figure this out," rather than the more common, "I'm going to have to ask my teacher how this goes".

For the above reasons, it is vitally important that teachers *never tell their students how long half notes are*. Telling students the value of half notes is, basically speaking, insulting their intelligence. The teachers are doing the thinking and the students are passively listening. When it comes to figuring out the value of half notes, students are eminently able to do that on their own, and we in music need to give our students more opportunities to think for themselves. The only values that students need to know are the durations of the whole notes. This forces them to become independent learners so far as half notes are concerned. Instilling this kind of an attitude in students now results in students who become rhythmically independent thinkers later. Students who are challenged to do their own thinking and who consistently come up with the correct answers, develop a healthy sense of self-esteem. In education, self-esteem is the greatest of all motivators.

The chalkboard introduction to the theory of half notes is followed by teacher-made worksheets like the sample that follows. After half notes, quarters are introduced as notes that are one-half the value of half notes. Eighth notes are notes that are one-half the value of quarter notes, and sixteenth notes are notes that are one-half the value of eighth notes. Using this model allows students to deal exclusively with one mathematical function -- the value of one-half. It makes everything extremely easy and manageable. Students are taught to chant,

Whole, Half, Quarter, Eighth, Sixteenth
8   4   2   1   1/2

Note: For a more in-depth look at this process, readers may want to read the *Conductor Score* to David Newell's complete rhythm theory book for young band students entitled, *The Simple Rhythmatician (Neil A. Kjos Music Company; 2007. W38F).*

Sample Worksheet
******

♩ Half Notes ♩

Adding a **stem** (|) to the side of an oval-shaped notehead (either ♩ or ♩) produces the second member of the *Family of Notes* -- the **half note**.

There are two very important things to know about half notes.

> • They are *always* called half notes. That will *never* change.
>   √ ♩ and ♩ are half notes.
>   √ No matter how many counts they get, the name stays the same.
>
> • Half notes receive *one-half* as many counts as whole notes.
>   √ That is why they are called half notes.
>
> | If o =100 | If o = 20 | If o = 8 | If o = 4 |
> |---|---|---|---|
> | then ♩ = 50 | then ♩ = 10 | then ♩ = 4 | then ♩ = 2 |

Most of the notes in the following exercises are half notes.
- • You will be given only the number of counts whole notes are worth.
- • *It is your job to figure out how long the half notes need to be*.

How did you do on those three exercises? If you played them correctly, you probably thought something like this:

Continue thinking the same way: "Whole, half; _?_, _?_ "

5 **Merrily We Roll Along**   Traditional

6 **Twinkle, Twinkle Little Star**   Wolfgang Amadeus Mozart

> *Note: When asked to calculate "one-half of one," many young students will respond "zero." A question such as, "I have one candy bar; if I give you half of it, are you really going to get zero (no) candy?" can help them to realize that one-half of one is actually one-half. *It is important that students understand this.*

Summary: Half Notes

As was stated earlier, the half note lesson is one of the more important ones for students to master. Students who successfully complete this unit have learned that the duration of half notes is not something to be memorized and remembered. Rather, half note durations can simply be reasoned, and this figuring out how long half notes are is a very easy task for the students. Students who do well at any subject become self-motivated to continue learning that subject. Rhythm becomes one of the favorite parts of their musical studies. All human beings enjoy feeling competent. A feeling of competence is the most important of all rewards. It is an internal, intrinsic reward bestowed upon the student by the student. So much more important and longer lasting than a piece of candy.

The teacher and the worksheets never tell the students the value of half notes, but instead always tell them only the value of the whole notes. Because of that, students begin to learn by direct experience that rhythmic problems are their responsibility. The fact that this process of discovering the durations of half notes is so logical and simple and easy goes a long way toward debunking the idea that musical rhythm is something mysterious that they will *someday* come to understand. Students who give half notes three counts because the whole notes are six counts in a certain etude have a complete and logical understanding of how rhythm works, even though they will never see a six-count whole note in "real" music. However, these same students will also not be at all confused, upset, or concerned when they are later introduced to "real" music in which whole notes are two counts! When the time comes to formally introduce them to cut time, they will need only to be shown that the symbol ₵ stands for the fact that whole notes are two counts. With that simple introduction to cut time, they will easily sight-read through the cut time section of their method book with complete understanding of why the half notes are one count. When whole notes are six counts, half notes are three. When whole notes are four counts, half notes are two. When whole notes are two counts, half notes are one. It all makes perfect sense to them. They figured it out for themselves.

The 30-second Cut Time Lesson

Teacher: Please turn in your books to page 17. Does anyone see anything new on this page?

Brian:	There's something that looks sort of like a capital letter C with a line down through it where the time signature goes.
Teacher:	Right, Brian. Does everyone see that? It's right before the first note in the exercise. *He draws one on the chalkboard to make certain that all the students are looking at the correct symbol.* Well, I'll be telling you more about this sign over the next few lessons, but I know you want to get playing right now, so I'm going to tell you everything you need to know in order to play this new page.
	This new sign simply means that whole notes are two counts. That's all there is to it. Whole notes are two counts. Any questions? Good. Let's play number one.

******

The students will play the page without difficulty or confusion or concern. They completely understand everything they need to know when whole notes are two counts. They have done it numerous times. They find the music to be easy, because the writer of the book thought that this idea of cut time would be difficult for them to grasp, so he or she wrote easy tunes and rhythms. The writer did not know, of course, that these particular students already knew all about cut time, except for the fact that they had never heard the term "cut time," and they had never seen the symbol to represent it. But they knew the most important thing about it. They knew how to do it. Their teacher had given them all the tools needed to begin the new unit in their books with an immediate sense of accomplishment. They feel good about cut time. It's exciting and energizing to start a new unit in your book and to zip right through it.

Whole Note Durations in Students' *Other* Music

As students become more accepting of the idea that whole note durations are changeable, some may inquire about the value of the whole notes in their "real" music. If the subject comes up, students can simply be told to "look at the bottom number of the time signature." When the bottom number is four, which it will be in most cases, the whole note equals four counts. *The bottom number of the time signature indicates the value of the whole note*. If students are playing music in cut time, they will need to know that the bottom number of the time signature for cut time is 2. Therefore, whole notes equal two counts in cut time.

Solving for X

In order to arrive at all of the correct answers in an algebra formula such as the one we are discussing, it is only necessary to discover the value of *x*. Once *x* is known, all other values can be determined, because their values are completely based on their relationship to *x*. The whole note is music's *x* and is the key that unlocks rhythm's mysteries for young students. How does the young music student determine the value of music's *x*? For students it is extremely easy. For teachers it may be more difficult. Adults will need to embrace a new definition of the meanings of the numbers in time signatures, and radical change is never easy. For the benefit of young students, however, this new definition needs to replace the centuries-old definition that we all know. The older, traditional definition will be added later, but young students are far more likely to gain an *instant understanding* of rhythm theory, if they are first taught this new definition.

> **Readers are strongly encouraged to keep an open mind and to withhold judgment on the following ideas until they have read all of the supporting materials that follow.**

In order to determine whether the whole note *(x)* is two counts or four counts or eight counts and so on, *students simply need to look at the bottom number of the time signature*. If the bottom number is four, they can easily be taught to understand that whole notes are four, half notes are two, and quarter notes are one. The only math involved is knowing what half of something is, and the vast majority of third and fourth graders can do that with ease. If they see that the bottom number of the time signature is sixteen, they simply think, *'whole, half, quarter, eighth, sixteenth; 16,8,4,2,1.'* When it is eight, they think, *'whole, half, quarter, eighth, sixteenth; 8,4,2,1, 1/2.'*

X = the bottom number of the time signature.

Such a radical departure from the traditional explanation of the meaning of the bottom number in time signatures deserves not only an explanation of its origins, but also some sort of empirical validation that it works with students.

The Story of the Bottom Number: The Origins

I was teaching one of my elementary instrumental classes one day, a class of approximately fifteen sixth grade students who met twice a week for thirty minutes. I had taught the students as beginners, and so they were totally comfortable with the concept of changeable count whole notes. At some time during most class meetings, they had been reminded that whole notes are not necessarily four counts. On any given day, for instance, I might ask to hear their warm-up scale "in quarter notes--- whole notes are sixteen." No other information relative to note values would be given. They had been taught to simply think for themselves: *whole, half, quarter -- 16,8,4*. They found the math to be terribly easy. Each new value was half of the one before it. They were proud of the fact that they were figuring out the note values on their own. They felt empowered, because they were doing the thinking. In so many classrooms it seems that the teachers are the only ones who are thinking! This particular class, however, had been doing only traditional work out of their method book for a fairly long time. This meant that all of the quarter notes they had been seeing for quite a while had been one count. I decided that day to warm them up with some whole notes of differing values just to remind them once again, through performance, that note values are not set in stone. I went back several pages in the book and found some simple etudes that were composed of whole, half, and quarter notes written in 2/4 and 4/4 time. I told the students that I was going to change some things on these review studies and that I was going to give them very little time to think about the changes. This was to be a test of how "quick" they were. Students love such challenges.

The first simple etude was written in 2/4 and consisted entirely of half notes. I said, very rapidly and without pause while snapping the tempo with my fingers, "Instruments up. Get ready. Whole notes are six -- ready, play," and the students instantly played each half note for three counts, thereby confirming their understanding of the rhythmic theory involved. This was followed by a few more similar etudes, each with different whole note values. All were done flawlessly, with the students showing obvious pleasure at their quickness.

It was time to end the warm-up period and so I announced the final etude, got their instruments up into playing position, snapped the tempo and said, "Ready, -" but before I could say "play," Katherine interrupted with, "Mr. Newell --." Everyone took their instruments out of playing position, and I responded with, "Yes, Katherine?"

"You forgot to tell us how long whole notes are!"

Indeed, something had distracted me and I had forgotten to give them a new whole note value for this final warm-up etude. Without having planned to do so and, to my knowledge, without ever having consciously thought through it, I more or less just blurted out, "Do you want to know how composers tell you how long whole notes are?" The response was an enthusiastic and immediate, "Yes!" to which I replied, "That's what the bottom number of the time signature really means. In this case the bottom number is four, and so it's *whole, half, quarter -- 4,2,1."* The review period ended with the students playing the printed 4/4 etude as written, and the class continued on with the assigned lesson for the day.

Immediately after class, I somewhat nervously sat down and thought through several different time signatures, hoping that what I had told the students was true in all cases, not just in the 2/4 and 4/4 examples they had played during this particular warm-up. To my relief, I was able to confirm that it worked for all simple time signatures. I reasoned that in 12/8, for example, if students are taught that the bottom number tells them that whole notes are eight counts, then half notes are four, quarter notes are two, and eighth notes are one. That, of course, is what the traditional method tells us. We were all taught that the bottom number of the time signature, in this case an eight, stands for the kind of note that receives one count.

Because they grasped the new concept so readily, from that day forward I taught all my students, including those in the secondary schools, that the bottom number of the time signature tells them how many counts the whole note gets. My problems helping students to understand and remember the meanings of the numbers in time signatures were virtually ended. (We are discussing only *simple meters* here. Compound meters are discussed later).

A Study To Validate The Theory

At approximately the same time that I blundered my way onto this new interpretation of the bottom numbers of time signatures, I was beginning my Master of Arts in Education degree and was taking the obligatory "Research" course. As part of the course, I was given the option of running a small, unofficial study, and I decided that this was a perfect opportunity to test the effectiveness of this new concept with a wider audience than just my classes. With the aid of three other teachers in the school district, a study involving 172 students in grades four through seven from four different school buildings was conducted. Of the four teachers, two were instrumental teachers with seventeen and thirteen years experience respectively, one was a vocal teacher with seven years experience, and the last was a 4th grade classroom teacher, who had been a music major for her first two years of college and who taught music to both of the 4th grade classes in her school. She agreed to teach one of her classes the traditional interpretation of the numbers in time signatures and the other would receive the experimental treatment. The two instrumental teachers included both first and second year classes in the study. The vocal teacher chose a morning and an afternoon section of 7th grade choir.

At an organizational meeting, an equal number of each teacher's classes were assigned to receive either the traditional or the experimental interpretation of the meanings of the numbers in time signatures. Although the assigning of classes to either group was totally random, with class names having been pulled out of a box, the resulting sizes of the two groups were fairly even in the number of students. Eighty-nine students received the traditional treatment and the experimental group numbered eighty-three.

At the beginning of the experiment, the students took a short, unannounced pretest, which is reproduced below:

1) 4/4 𝅝 = ___ counts.	6) 3/4 ♩ = ___ counts.
2) 8/16 𝅗𝅥 = ___ counts.	7) 8/8 𝅝 = ___ counts.
3) 2/2 𝅝 = ___ counts.	8) 6/4 ♪ = ___ counts.
4) 3/8 ♪ = ___ counts.	9) 3/2 𝅗𝅥 = ___ counts.
5) 4/1 𝅝 = ___ counts.	10) 1/4 ♩ = ___ counts.

Following the administration of the pretest, each class received three ten-minute lessons on three different days relative to the meanings of the numbers in time signatures. The traditional students were taught the centuries-old meaning, that the top number indicates the number of counts in a measure and the bottom number stands for the kind of note that receives one count. The experimental groups also learned that the top number indicates the number of counts in a measure, but that the bottom number indicates the value of the whole note. A post-test, which was the exact same test as the pretest but with the test items in a scrambled order, was then administered and scored to determine the degree of improvement between pretest and post-test for each group.

As one would expect, no student scored a perfect 10/10 on the unannounced pretest. Of the eighty-nine students who received the traditional explanation of the meanings of the numbers in time signatures, *7% of the students scored a perfect 10/10* on the post-test. Students in those classes raised their score an average of almost one point out of ten (+.94), clearly demonstrating that learning did occur. The improvement did not appear to be that dramatic, however, considering the fact that the students had three ten-minute lessons on the subject.

Of the eighty-three students who received the explanation that the bottom number of the time signature indicates the duration of the whole note, a startling *52% of the students scored a perfect 10/10* on the post-test. Students in the experimental groups improved their score between pretest and post-test by +4.55 out of 10.

At a get-together of the teachers after the study was completed, during which the results were shared with them, the 4th grade classroom teacher said, "I have to tell you something. I didn't follow your directions exactly with the experimental group. I just didn't need ten minutes on the third session with them. They were answering every question that I put to them, and so we just went on to something else." At that, one of the other teachers looked at me, nodded and said, "Same here."

Conclusions

How is this possible? How could the students in the experimental classes, approximately 30% of whom were 4th graders, learn this material in such a superior fashion and in less time? Fifty-two percent perfect papers compared to seven percent perfect papers is, in my view, statistically important. There are probably multiple answers to this question, but the following two seem to me to be especially significant.

(1) When compared to the traditional method, this new approach is so much simpler to teach and to understand. Traditionally we ask young students to look at two numbers, one over the other, but only the top number is actually interpreted as a number. The top *number* indicates the *number of counts* in a measure, but the bottom number doesn't represent a number at all. It stands for *a kind of a note*.

When students are first introduced to time signatures, the bottom number is almost certainly a four. I am personally unaware of any beginning music book that first introduces students to 2/2 or 6/8 or any meters other than 2/4 or 4/4. And so the first task in helping students to decipher the meaning of the bottom number is getting them to realize that the "4" represents a quarter note. Experience has demonstrated to many teachers that this may not be as easy as it sounds. Students first need to learn that the four represents the fraction 1/4. They then have to understand that, of all the fractions that exist, this is the only one that is regularly pronounced two different ways, both as *one-fourth* and as *a quarter*. This could very well be another new thing for some students to learn, thereby complicating the teaching even more. The number "4" does not represent a *fourth note,* as many young students will say. Once students understand that the bottom number in 4/4 represents a quarter note, they then have to remember what it is about the quarter note that is so important. This is the kind of note that receives one count. There is nothing in the time signature to remind them of that fact. It simply must be memorized. Finally, they have to plug this one-count information into the middle of the hierarchy of notes, which is where the quarter note resides. In other words, to calculate values for all of the notes in the piece, students are forced to perform two different mathematical procedures. Some notes are *twice as much* as others, and some are *half as much.* These closely related concepts of *half as much* and *twice as much* are very difficult for many young students to comprehend.

Given the mental gymnastics just described, is it any wonder that many young students just don't get it, and that many of those who do don't see the value in it? Since the students already *know* that quarter notes are one count anyway, why go through all those confusing steps? To most students, being taught to interpret the numbers in time signatures is just so much time-consuming "teacher babble." It's the kind of thing that gives the term "music theory" such a bad connotation in students' minds. It seems irrelevant to them, having little or nothing to do with their performance.

The experimental method is infinitely simpler and more logical and, therefore, easier to understand. Both numbers in time signatures represent exactly what they are --numbers; the *number* of counts in a measure and the *number* of counts in a whole note. When introducing this new concept to students, visual cues such as $\frac{|4|}{④}$ can help students to remember which number is which. The top number represents the number of counts in a measure (between barlines) and the bottom number represents the number of counts in a whole note. And finally, once the bottom number of the signature is *read* (it doesn't have to be *interpreted*), the mathematical calculation is always the same -- *Whole, half, quarter, eighth, sixteenth; bottom number, half, half, half, half.* So simple.

(2)   In my view, however, the principal reason that this new definition of the meanings of the numbers in time signatures works so well has to do with the system of rhythmic notation itself. There can be little doubt that the system that has evolved over the past few centuries is based absolutely on the whole note. The fact that this new definition identifies the value of the whole note makes it completely compatible with the system as it was designed. Our system of rhythmic notation is, without a doubt, the "Whole Note System."

The Whole Note System

Absolutely everything about our system of rhythmic notation is derived from and dependent upon the whole note. As the whole note goes, so goes the system.

(1)   The whole note is the genesis of all of the note symbols themselves. Not all notes have stems, or are filled in, or have flags or beams, but all of the basic notes retain the original oval shape of the whole note from which they descended. "In the beginning was the whole note...."

(2)   All note names are derived from their relationship to the whole note. Students can be shown that, when the notes are referred to by their "full names," the individual members of the family of notes all have the same last name.

> --------------*half* of a **whole note**
> ----------*quarter* of a **whole note**
> -----------*eighth* of a **whole note**
> ------- *sixteenth* of a **whole note**

(3)   All note values are absolutely dependent upon the value of the whole note. Traditionally in 4/4 time, the quarter note is identified as the note that gets one count, but that identification does not *cause* the note to be one count. The quarter note is not one count in a certain piece because the time signature says so. The root cause of the quarter note's one-count value is the fact that the whole note is four counts. That is the only way that the name "quarter note" makes any sense. Philosophers may long argue about which came first, the chicken or the egg, but we can definitely know which came first, the quarter

note or the whole note. A quarter of anything validates the prior, theoretical existence of the whole thing. Rhythmically speaking, there is no doubt that the whole note is the first and the foremost of all notational elements, and students who understand that the value of the whole note can change from piece to piece will necessarily understand why all note values are changeable from piece to piece. By far, the most important note value for students to know is the value of the whole note. And where do they find this information? They can simply read the bottom number of the time signature.

Why The One-Count Note?

Why, then, are we so transfixed on the kind of note that gets one count? Historically speaking, the importance of identifying the one-count note was immense. In the Medieval period, what we today call *the beat* in music was then called *the tactus*. Gaffurius (*Practica musice*, 1496) wrote that the *tactus* equalled the pulse of a man breathing normally, suggesting a tempo of 60 to 70 beats per minute (bpm). Music scholars believe that during medieval times, it was common practice that this *tempo* or *tactus* never varied. The tempo remained unchanged from piece to piece. Therefore, if the composer wanted one piece of music to be faster than another, instead of changing the tempo, he simply changed the kind of note that received the tactus beat. A modern day example of this might be a first piece of music written in 4/4 at a tempo of 120 bpm and a second piece written in 2/2, also at a tempo of 120 bpm. If the music in both pieces consisted solely of whole notes and half notes, the tempo would remain the same for both pieces, but the music in the 2/2 piece would sound twice as fast. In medieval times it was imperative that the performer knew what kind of note was to receive one count -- the *tactus note*.

This practice is actually the derivation of our modern day cut time, more formally known as *alla breve*. In medieval times, music was mostly written in what is referred to as "white notation," meaning that note symbols were not filled in. The equivalent of our modern day half note, the *minum*, was actually the shortest of all the note symbols, which explains the absence of black ink. Although it seems highly unusual to us, the kind of note that very often received one count was the equivalent of our modern day whole note, known as the *semibreve*. There was actually a time signature named *alla semibreve,* meaning that the semibreve (our whole note) was the kind of note to receive one count. When composers wanted to write faster music, they indicated that the *tactus* note should be the note twice as long as the semibreve, which was the *breve*. The breve is the equivalent of our seldom

112

seen double whole note. This change of the one-count note to the larger breve, of course, had the same effect upon the music. The music moved twice as fast while the tempo, the tactus, stayed the same. The term *alla breve* literally means *in the time of the breve*.

The Derivation of Cut Time *(alla breve)* Using Modern Notational Equivalents

Tactus = 60-70

The one-count note is still important to modern musicians when it comes to setting the tempo, but no involved interpretation is required. With the patenting of the metronome by Johann Nepomuk Maelzel in 1815, composers could finally indicate the exact tempo at which they envisioned their music being performed. Metronome markings today clearly indicate the kind of note that receives one count. By reading such signs as ♩ = 80 performers today can know not only what kind of note is to receive one count, but they can also know the precise tempo the composer had in mind as the piece was being written. Having the bottom number of the time signature identify the kind of note that receives one count is not nearly as important today as it once was. Having the bottom number indicate the value of the whole note yields a great deal more important information in a more simple and understandable way. Presenting important information to young learners in a simple and understandable way is one of the keys to success.

An Objection To This New Definition

Whenever this different interpretation of the bottom number of the time signature has been presented at workshops, in methods classes, or to individuals, the following objection has occasionally been voiced:

"Wait a minute. You're asking me to teach my students that in 2/4, there are two counts in a measure and a whole note is four counts. *But in 2/4, there is no such thing as a whole note!"*

In my view, this objection is raised by people who simply haven't had enough time to step back and think through the whole process. If there is no whole note, there is no system. There has to be a whole note. The very term "half note" validates the existence of the whole note. Mathematically speaking, the person who says that there is no such thing as a whole note is basically saying that a whole note equals zero. If that is true, then a half note equals one-half of zero, which is zero. A quarter note equals one-fourth of zero, which is zero, and so forth. I repeat -- without the whole note we have no system of rhythmic notation. By the way, no student has ever raised this question to me -- only adults.

The composer who writes a piece of music in 2/4 is basically saying to the performers: "I am putting two counts worth of notes in every measure in this piece, *based on a whole note value of four*. Although you won't see the symbol of a whole note anywhere in the piece, all of the notes that you do see are based on a whole note value of four. And by the way, if I want you to *sound* the equivalent of a whole note, I will tie together a half plus a half which, of course, equals a whole."

My students and I used to call such music "Base 4 Music" -- music *based* on a whole note value of four. Similarly, we called music in 4/2 or 3/2 or 2/2 and the like "Base 2 Music" -- music based on a whole note value of two. It was understood that the whole note must always exist, whether seen or not, because from its value, all other note values are derived.

Conclusions

And so it is up to us. We can continue to go through the multiple and often confusing steps required to try to get students to understand the centuries-old definition of the bottom number of the time signature which, once accomplished, reveals information that to most students doesn't seem to be terribly important. Or we can make it extremely simple, instantly yielding information that enables even the youngest of students to comprehensively understand the fundamental structure of the entire system of rhythmic notation.

Changing our thinking relative to the bottom number of the time signature may not be easy for many of us, but the benefits to the world's future musicians could be significant and well worth the effort. Those of you who are not yet convinced are urged to run your own comparative studies. The impressive improvement in understanding and the positive feelings of self esteem demonstrated by students who are figuring out rhythmic facts for themselves could very well convince even the most doubtful among you. The key to having young students understand the underlying algebraic formula that is the system of rhythmic notation sits innocently on the page in front of them. It is the bottom number of the time signature.

Teaching the Traditional Meaning of the Bottom Number

The way that we traditionally introduce students to rhythmic notation and time signatures does not work very well, because it challenges them to think in ways that are developmentally beyond most of them. Through years of experience with musical note symbols, they have come to the conclusion that the musical symbol known as the whole note does not *represent* the number "4" in their songs. To their concrete thinking brains, it actually *is* the number "4." Although they most likely wouldn't put it into these words, they probably feel that there is a good reason why those who devised the system didn't just write the numeral "4" on the manuscript whenever a four-count sound was wanted. It would be too difficult to tell whether the "4" was on a line or in a space. So, they decided to disguise the "4" as a nice oval shaped symbol that could easily position itself on the staff. With that kind of a mind-set, young students are not easily able to understand how that same symbol can also represent other numbers. That kind of thinking is too complicated for young minds and, most importantly, students do not consider it to be worth their time. However, students who are introduced to the concept that the bottom number of the time signature indicates the value of the whole note, and who are given the opportunity to actually sing and play whole notes of many different values early in their studies, have a thorough and complete understanding of the basic structure of rhythmic notation.

Make no mistake about it. Students do eventually need to be taught the traditional meaning of the bottom numbers in time signatures in order to function in the musical world. *This does not create a problem.* Students who have received a thorough grounding in the system that is advocated here have no difficulty assimilating both definitions into one cohesive package when they are older and are able to view things from more than one perspective. Young children become confused when they hear someone refer to an American unit of measure as "a foot" in one sentence and "12 inches" in the next. They do not understand that they are the same measurement. As they mature in their thinking and experience, of course, they understand completely that this is simply two ways of stating the same thing. They very likely don't even realize that the measurement was described in two different ways, because they understand both. So, too, with the bottom numbers of time signatures. When they are more mature, students can look at the bottom number of a simple time signature and realize that it represents both the value of the whole note, and it signifies the kind of note that gets one count at the same time. In fact, the two definitions actually validate each other. When the bottom number is four, they know that whole notes are four counts, half notes are two and, of course, quarter notes are one count. There is no conflict. Students are free to think about it from whichever perspective they prefer. However, when it comes time for students to understand the meanings of the numbers in *compound* time signatures, they will need to know that the bottom number of the time signature stands for a kind of a note.

Students ideally need to know both definitions of the bottom numbers of time signatures. We are not suggesting that the traditional definition be replaced, just *deferred* until students' minds can better comprehend it. The significant advantage of the new definition is that it speaks a language that the very youngest of students can understand. It starts them on the road to rhythmic competence with a feeling of confidence.

Part Three

A Discussion
of
Counting Systems
in
Simple Meters

Up to this point in the book, I have purposely illustrated many different counting systems. When discussing the counting of four sixteenths in 4/4 meter, for example, they were variously called *Mis-sis-sip-pi, Du-ta-de-ta, Ti-ri-ti-ri, 1-e-&-a,* and so forth. One of the most important and overriding themes throughout this text has been the idea that our students must be given the luxury of being able to concentrate on only one thing at a time. I did not want to give the impression that you should change your own, favorite counting system as you worked your way through *The Rhythm Learning Sequence* with your students. That would create an unnecessary distraction for students. Students who have been taught that the counting words for four quarter notes in 4/4 are *Ta Ta Ta Ta* do not need to change to *1 2 3 4,* or *Du Du Du Du,* or anything else in order to understand the concepts advanced in the book. They simply need to concentrate on their own teacher's *Ta Ta Ta Ta* language. You are encouraged to use the counting system that works best for you, with the understanding that your students need to be given the time necessary to master that counting language *before* they are expected to associate it with printed notation. The language before the look. The counting language is best learned when we say to our students, *"Would you like to see what* Ta Ta Ta Ta *looks like in notes?"* The sequence is far more important than the particular language. Youngsters in France learn to speak *French* so well, not because it is an easier or better language than *English.* They master *French* because of the way they are introduced to it. They learn to speak it before they are asked to associate it with something on a printed page. Young music students do not learn to speak *Du-ta-de-ta* so well because it is either a better or an easier language than *1-e-&-a.* They master their own particular rhythm language because of the way they are introduced to it. They learn to speak it before they are asked to read it. It's the method that matters. Any counting language will be successful if it is mastered before it is associated with any particular written symbols, and if it is used consistently.

Counting systems are enormously important to the rhythmic education of students. They are prevalent in the profession. Although I am not personally aware of any study or survey that has been conducted on the subject, I would be surprised to find very many music teachers who do not advocate some sort of a counting system in their practice. The *Rhythm Learning Sequence* advocated in this book places a very high priority on the establishment of a system of vocalizing rhythmic sounds. Step Two in the sequence is named "Count It." Counting allows students to first perform the rhythms using the instruments on which they are the most accomplished -- their speaking voices. They have been successfully using these instruments for many years, and they certainly do not have to think about how to form their lips or where to put their tongues when saying their counting words. Their speaking voices are truly automatic instruments by now, allowing them to concentrate exclusively on the rhythmic sounds they are speaking. Once they have told themselves how the rhythms sound using the *speaking* instruments that they mastered long ago, they then simply have to transfer the same sounds to their newer, *musical* instruments. Logically this makes a great deal of sense, proceeding from the most simple to the slightly more complex, from the well-known instruments to the less well-known.

All that being said, I will be advocating for one particular type of counting system. I realize that many of us are totally dedicated to our chosen counting systems. It is absolutely not my intention to try to change anyone's mind in that regard. I know that in many cases that would not be possible, nor would it be desirable. My intention is simply to share some insights into counting systems with the hope of broadening all of our understandings relative to this important teaching tool. Those of you who are totally happy with and committed to your particular system may very well want to skip this part of the book. *"If it ain't broke, don't fix it"* comes to mind. However, if you press on and read the material that follows, you may actually reap an unexpected benefit. As human beings, we cannot know how good something really is until we have the opportunity to compare it to something that is not as good. So, as you energetically disagree with every assertion that is made here about counting systems, you will become more convinced than ever that your particular system is the better one. After reading this material, you will continue using your counting system with renewed vigor, confident in its ability to help your students achieve rhythmically in a way that is superior to all others. Your convictions will be strengthened and you will be a better teacher of your own counting system because of it.

For pre-service music teachers with no teaching experience, and for experienced teachers who have used one or several systems and find yourselves not particularly attached to any one of them, perhaps this discussion can help to clarify the principles you might want to consider when deciding on a counting system. The discussion will center itself mainly around three ideas: (1) Rhythm's *Lyrics*, (2) The Use of Numbers in Counting Systems, and (3) Putting Rhythms Into Space.

Rhythm's *Lyrics*

A few years ago I had the opportunity to evaluate a high school band program. I observed three full days at the school. It was agreed that the first visit would be as informal as possible. I would simply come and sit through the full day's schedule of band rehearsals, notice what there was to notice, ask questions if I had them, and generally just get a taste of the students and the school environment. I would not do any kind of an evaluation on the initial visit. On the second and third visits the following week, a video recorder would be set up, and I would add formal "play-by-play" commentary onto the tape as the rehearsals were progressing.

I first observed one of the two concert bands in the high school. This was a group of approximately sixty 10th, 11th, and 12th graders who, by audition, had been placed into the second-level band. After a couple of warm-up scales and chord studies, the students were instructed to get up their "rhythm sheet," a piece of paper on which was written a large number of rhythms. The rhythms were written without a staff and each complete measure was numbered consecutively. The assignment for this particular day was to play measures 9-16. The exercise was to be played on the Concert Bb Major Scale. Measure 9 was to be played on concert Bb, measure 10 on concert C, and so forth.

Before playing the exercise, the students were asked to count all eight measures aloud. The counting language used was the well-known *1-e-&-a* counting system. The measures were counted very well, with complete confidence and clarity of diction. It was clear to me that the entire class was counting the rhythms. This was not one of those situations in which ten students were really counting and the remaining students were mumbling something that resembled counting. These students could count! I was very impressed. But then a strange thing happened. They couldn't play the exercise. The group had to stop and "work out" at least three of the eight measures individually before trying to put it back together as a complete exercise. Even with all of the attention given the three individual measures, the final run-through of all eight measures was not very good.

This really puzzled me. How could the students count the measures perfectly but have so much trouble playing them? I temporarily decided that this might be one of the reasons that these students didn't get placed in the school's top band. They were the least experienced students in the high school program, and their performance would hopefully improve over time. However, when the school's top band came and was given the same type of exercise, the results were basically identical. These students counted aloud as well as or better than the first group, but they also couldn't play what they counted. Even when working on an individual measure, the students had difficulty playing it correctly immediately after counting it aloud. It was clear that the students in this band program couldn't *play* what they could *say*. By now, however, I had a fairly good idea of what the problem was.

One, *and ONLY ONE*, Word or Syllable for Each Printed Musical Symbol

We need to explain to our students over and over again *the reason* that we teach them to count rhythms. Many students who can count rhythms do not really know why they were taught to do that. They probably assume that counting rhythms is just something that you do when you learn to read music. We need to make it perfectly clear to our students that *we teach them to count so they can independently figure out rhythms without our help*. Psychologically, most students readily buy into the program when it is explained in those terms. One of the primary drives of young people is to become independent of adults. They strive mightily to do things for themselves. "I'd rather do it myself" is a universal mantra of youth. Counting rhythms helps our students to achieve that goal rhythmically. When they are practicing alone, they can look at a rhythm, tell themselves what it sounds like by saying it aloud, and then simply play or sing the rhythmic sounds that they just vocalized. They don't need us, and that is good for everyone. *Look, Say, and Perform*. But this simple regimen does not work too well if what the students say sounds different from what they are supposed to play or sing. What they say with their speaking voices must be echoed exactly by their musical voices.

Students who look at a whole note in 4/4 time and who count aloud, "*1, 2, 3, 4*" are demonstrating that they *understand* that the note receives four counts, which is all well and good. However, the purpose of counting rhythms is *not* to demonstrate understanding. *The purpose of counting is to model the rhythm's performance*.

The whole note does not sound ☐☐☐☐. Therefore, it should not be counted "*1, 2, 3, 4*" -- four separate vocal sounds. Uttering four separate sounds in this case does not serve the purpose of counting aloud. It is no help whatsoever. Clearly, students need to understand that the note receives four counts *before* they attempt to read it for performance. It cannot be stated too strongly. The purpose of counting is not to demonstrate understanding; it is to model performance. A whole note in 4/4 time must be counted as follows if the counting is to model the anticipated performance and be helpful to students seeking rhythmic independence:

$$\frac{4}{4} \quad \mathbf{o} \quad \Big| \qquad \text{or} \qquad \frac{4}{4} \quad \mathbf{o} \quad \Big|$$
$$\quad 1 \text{———} \qquad\qquad\qquad Du \text{———}$$

or any other *sustained, continuous, one-sound vocalization*.

We need to be teaching our students to *say* rhythms the way they will *sing or play* them. If students are to imitate the sounds of their counting performances, then the counting performances must reflect the notation, not the notation's underlying structure. One note, one sound. The counting words that they vocalize should be thought of as the rhythm's "lyrics," and the lyrics must fit exactly with the notation.

A composer setting the word *"over"* to music will write two notes, because the word has two syllables. A composer who would set the word to just one note is not helping the performer to know how to sing the word.

The singer sees the following lyric under a half note:

How is it to be sung?

The performer has no idea how to sing the note and must simply make an educated guess. If for some reason the composer actually wanted the word to be sung on one note, he or she would need to change the word. The words and/or syllables of words must be a perfect fit with the notation.

In vocal music, except where slurs and ties are involved, there is a one-to-one correspondence of words or syllables to printed notes. All of our students, both vocal and instrumental, would benefit from the fanciful idea that every piece of music includes an *unwritten set of lyrics*. These lyrics are the rhythm's counting words. Just like actual song lyrics, these unseen lyrics also consist of one word or syllable for every printed note on the page. They help students to independently unlock the mystery of the rhythmic sounds intended. If they can say the counting lyrics to a steady beat, then they can play or sing the rhythm. For the students, it becomes basically *"My turn, my turn: I will first recite the rhythm's lyrics aloud, and then I will echo those same sounds musically."* In effect, the students *teach themselves*, which is one of the surest signs that real education has occurred. One of a teacher's most important goals is to be no longer needed. Having our students say the rhythm's lyrics is a powerful teaching tool, provided the lyrics reflect precisely the rhythm's performance.

The bands that I saw during that first day of observations counted aloud very well, demonstrating that they probably *understood* the rhythms. However, their performance clearly demonstrated that their counting was not helping them to play the rhythms. That is because their counting lyrics did not consistently match the written notation. Only in measures 11, 13, and 15 below did the counting sound like the notation.

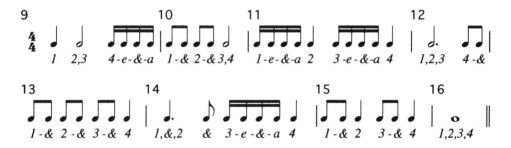

During lunch and after school that first day, this topic was discussed at considerable length. On my second visit one week later, it became instantly clear to me that the bands' counting system had been amended. The bands did a rhythm sheet exercise that day also, but with impressively different results. They counted the assigned measures using only one word or syllable for each printed symbol, and they played the exercise virtually error free. Their counting informed them exactly how the music was supposed to sound. As they played the etude, they could have been silently *singing the lyrics in their heads* for a perfect match. Although they did eight different measures that second day, I have reprinted the same measures 9-16 below, so that the difference in the counting systems can be clearly discerned.

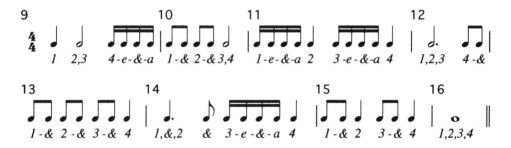

I asked the director how difficult it had been to switch the students to this different way of counting rhythms in such a short time. After all, they had been very thoroughly schooled in the other system. He reported that it took only a couple of days. A few students still might occasionally start to say more than one word for a single note, but they quickly remembered the new system and adjusted immediately without difficulty.

A *Counting* Language Is Also A *Musical* Language

In addition to using a counting system in which the words and the notes did not match one-for-one, the students in this band program counted unmusically. The following example of counting is rhythmically correct, but musically insensitive. More than just the sound of the rhythm's durations can be established in the recitation of a rhythm's lyrics.

Rhythm as written:

Rhythm as counted:

It is highly unlikely that any of us would want the quarter notes above to be performed in the style that they were counted! How much more musically meaningful to have the students recite the rhythm with a connected style of vocal articulation, resembling as closely as possible the way we would want such notes to sound as they are played or sung in our ensembles.

When we introduce our students to our counting language, we become, in effect, language teachers. *Our students will learn to speak the language as we speak it!* This is both a tremendous responsibility and a wonderful opportunity. We can teach them to speak the language either expressively or in a style that is musically unattractive. Every time we share our counting language with our students, we need to model *musicality*. Spoken rhythms have the potential to be musically invigorating and sensitive. The students will do as we do. Therefore, what we do is extremely important.

Teacher:	Listen and repeat: my turn, your turn. *He chants, using the neutral syllable* "Du:"	

Students:	*The student response is rhythmically accurate, but devoid of any expression:*	

Teacher:	No, no. That is **not** what I did. Listen carefully. Do **exactly** as I do. Imitate me in every detail. *He repeats the same pattern with the gentle crescendo to count three, followed by a dynamic taper to the end of the measure.*	

Students:	*The student response this time is not only rhythmically accurate, but it is also musically expressive.*	

Teacher: Good. Now play the rhythm up the Concert Bb Major Scale. Play it exactly as you just said it. *The complete scale is played accurately **and** expressively.*

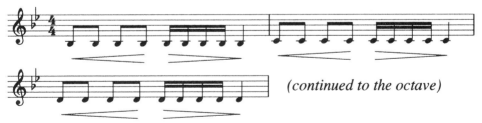

(continued to the octave)

Any counting language can teach more than just the mechanics of rhythm. It can teach musicianship as well. Rhythm is one of music's most expressive and exciting elements. Very often the flow of the rhythm determines the musical expression of the phrase. A single measure of rhythm like the one at the top of this page, even if only chanted, played, or sung on a single pitch, can be musically expressive. A melody is not an absolute requirement for making music. Students need to know that. It stands to reason that students who consistently *speak* rhythms expressively are far more likely to also *sing and play* them expressively. Our various counting languages and the way we use them can be potent tools in the development of musical expressiveness in our students. We need to always model musicality in the use of our own counting languages, and we must insist on in-kind responses from our students. Their responsibility is to imitate us with absolute fidelity. Our responsibility is to speak our counting languages musically. No rhythms -- spoken, sung, or played -- should be performed in our classrooms that do not have an expressive quality attached to them. As long as we are teaching students to count, we might as well teach them to count *musically*.

The Two Types of Counting Systems

All existing counting systems can be placed into one of two large groups: (1) those that use a combination of **numbers** and words or neutral syllables, and (2) those that use only words and neutral syllables, **no numbers**. Within each of these two categories there exists a tremendous variety of individual systems, but the differences among them are often insignificant. One system might prefer a certain set of words or neutral syllables, because of their relationship to instrumental articulations, for example. Another might choose a different vowel sound because of the way it shapes the inside of the mouth or the embouchure of a wind player. Overall, however, the most significant distinction between counting systems is in the use or the non-use of numbers. For reasons that I hope to make clear, I personally recommend a counting system that uses numbers.

The "1-e-&-a" System

If there was a single "inventor" of the counting system that uses both numbers and words, it seems as though many people have written *Variations on That Theme*. Number systems are very widely used, but in numerous versions. The different ways that single notes extending over more than one beat are counted has already been discussed at length. There are many other discrepancies. There is *1-& 2-&* versus *1-up 2-up*. There is *1-e-&-a* and *1-ta-ne-ta,* and many others.

To avoid confusion, the following is a very brief overview of *the specific version* of the 1-e-&-a number system that will be used here for purposes of illustration.

1. There is one, and only one, syllable associated with each printed note. Therefore, when the students recite the rhythm aloud correctly, they are hearing the exact sounds of the written notation.

2. Any note that is articulated on a beat is called by *the specific number of the beat* on which it occurs. A note that is articulated on count three in a measure is called *"3,"* no matter the time signature or the kind of note.

3. The first musical symbol in every full measure of music is called *"1,"* regardless of the kind of note or rest that it is and regardless of the time signature. Every full measure of music begins with *"1."*

4. Dividing a single beat into two equal sounds results in a second note, which is called either *and* or *an*, both pronounced exactly as they are in the English language. Most books print the word as *"&,"* but teachers and students writing the counts under rhythms most often use the mathematical *plus sign* -- *"+."*

5. When the single beat is subdivided into four equal parts, the words are *1-e-&-a* or *2-e-&-a* and so forth, depending upon the beat on which the figure occurs. The letter *"e"* is pronounced as it is in the English alphabet; *"a"* is pronounced *"uh,"* the same vowel sound as in the word *"other."* Notice the consistency provided by the fact that *the specific beat number* and the word *"&"* are always the words pronounced on the downbeats and on the upbeats.

6. When duple and quadruple subdivisions of the beat are combined on one beat, the lyrics retain all of the elements of the above vocabulary. Note that in a quadruple subdivision, the second and fourth notes each have their own individual names. In some counting systems, these two notes share the same name. In the *1-e-&-a* system, the second note is *"e"* and the fourth is *"a,"* allowing teachers to call specific attention to each individual subdivision of the four-note figure.

7. Triplets in simple meters are recited as *1-trip-let 2 trip-let,* and so forth. These lyrics are preferred to the perhaps more common *1-la-li 2-la-li* for the following simple reason. When students are trying to work out a rhythm on their own and they see the number *"3"* written above or below the triplet figure, they are more likely to recall the counting word *trip-let* than they are the neutral syllables *la-li.* "Triplet" seems to be the more logical choice. Students *see* triplet and they *say* "trip-let." Of course, the number identifies the count on which the triplet resides.

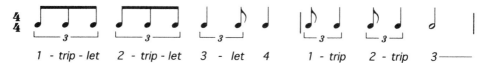

1 - trip - let   2 - trip - let   3 - let   4   1 - trip   2 - trip   3———

A counting suggestion for dividing triplet eighth notes into sixteenths is discussed in Part Four, *Teaching Compound Meter.*

A Final Note on this Particular Number Counting System

Having students always say the *specific number* on which a rhythmic figure is articulated is very important. The reasons for this will be discussed in detail shortly. However, when students are first introduced to the concept, they make a fair number of mistakes, but they are what we can call "good mistakes." Review is a powerful and necessary component in the mastery of new material with young learners, and when students make innocent and natural mistakes, we have a legitimate reason for spending a few seconds reviewing the new concept with them. The more they review it, the better they learn it.

When students are first introduced to the counting of two half notes in 4/4 time, for example, even though they correctly give each note two counts, they will very often make the following language error:

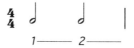

1——— 2———

When they see two things and they are asked to count them, it is natural for them to follow the number sequence that they have known since they first learned to talk. They have been reciting the counting series that begins *"1, 2, 3,"* for many years. When they hear themselves say *"1,"* they have to really concentrate to not follow that with *"2,"* especially given the fact that they are looking at two printed symbols, which each get two counts.

Teacher: Wait a minute, class. The first note in the measure is a half
              note. It uses up all of counts one and two, right? Therefore,
              the next note in the measure, no matter what kind of note it is,
              has to be on what count? Correct. It's on count three. Count
              two has been used up by the first note. It's gone. Let's count
              the measure again.

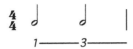

It does not take very long for students to become accustomed to the counting sounds of 1-3 or 1-4 or 2-4, and so forth. Even though at first glance it
may seem to be unnecessarily troublesome to subject young students to this
kind of "odd" counting, its importance cannot be stressed too strongly.

The Recommended System

One of the most important rehearsal skills for directors of performing
groups to master involves *pacing*. We must always strive to keep our students involved and active and participating in the process of making music.
It is imperative that we develop the ability to immediately hear problems
and to have strategies in mind to fix them quickly. The presence of this skill
is one of the most apparent differences between experienced and inexperi-
enced teachers. Those with less experience will eventually get the problems
solved. It just takes them longer to find and to fix the errors. The resulting
rehearsal down time creates boredom, invites discipline problems and a host
of other things, none of which are good. When rhythm errors occur, conductors who use a number counting system can often get to the root of the problem more quickly than others. Consider the following two scenarios:

(1) During the rehearsal, the students experience significant rhythmic diffi-
    culty with the following measure:

In an effort to quickly discover the problem, the director logically assumes
that it involves the most "difficult" rhythm in the measure, the four sixteenths. Wanting to solve the problem efficiently and get the rehearsal moving again, he asks:

Teacher: Class, how do you count the sixteenths in this measure?

Students: Du-ta-de-ta (or Ta-ka-di-mi or Ti-ri-ti-ri or any other non-number answer). *The students' response is immediate and confident. The teacher thinks, "They sure did that well. There's no doubt they understand. Maybe they just played them too slow or too fast. I'll have to listen more carefully this time."*

Teacher: That is correct. This time when we get to that spot, remember that. Make sure you actually play that sound. *When the students play the measure again, it sounds no better. The time consuming hunt for the solution to the problem begins.*

(2) Same scenario, different group. The students experience significant rhythmic difficulty with the same measure. In an effort to quickly find the problem, the director logically assumes that it lies with the most "difficult" rhythm in the measure, the four sixteenths.

Teacher: Class, how do you count the sixteenths in this measure?

Students: 2-e-&-a.

The basic problem is known instantly, because *the answer reveals the mistake.* There is no need to play the measure over and over in small groups of players until the root of the problem is discovered. The number-counting system has allowed the teacher to get inside the students' heads and to know precisely where their thinking has broken down. They simply need to be reminded that the half note is two counts. The sixteenths are on count three. They are counted *3-e-&-a,* not *2-e-&-a.* The problem was actually with the "easiest" rhythm in the measure, the half note. The reason the measure did not sound good was because at least some of the students played the sixteenths too soon, on count two. This immediate discovery of the problem was made possible because the students had been taught to use specific numbers that denote precisely where in the measure rhythmic figures reside. *Du-ta-de-ta* or *Ti-ri-ti-ri* or any of the numerous non-number systems do not yield this important information. Even though *Du-ta-de-ta* or *Mis-sis-sip-pi* or *Ti-ri-ti-ri* are correct answers to the question, they don't tell us very much about student comprehension of the structure of the particular measure being studied. They are *generalized* answers to a *specific* question. When students answer the above question with *3-e-&-a*, we know instantly and absolutely that they understand *these particular sixteenths*, which are the only ones that matter right now. Additionally, if they still cannot perform the measure correctly, we know that we are dealing with *a performance problem*, not a cognition problem. We can forgo the time-consuming process of trying to *explain* sixteenth notes to the students. They don't need that. We can proceed immediately to working on the performance aspects of the measure, making sure that the students wait until count three to play the sixteenths. With the answer to one quick and simple question, we discover immediately both the nature of the problem and the most direct path to take toward its solution.

This is not to suggest that students who offered a non-number answer do not understand the measure completely. Many of them probably do, but we have no way of actually knowing that without further time-consuming questioning, and time is the most precious commodity we have with our students. Solving problems quickly is an immensely important part of our skill package.

Bloom's Taxonomy of Cognitive Skills

In the 1950's, Benjamin Bloom and a group of leading educational psychologists developed a system for classifying the levels of thinking required of students in America's classrooms. Bloom's classification, which he gave the sophisticated label of a "taxonomy," identified six hierarchical levels of thinking. An example of the lowest level, that requiring the least thought, involves the simple recall of previously learned facts. Students are asked a question. They search their memory banks of already learned materials. They come up with the correct answer, and everyone is happy. Bloom's research indicated that 95% of the test questions being asked in the classroom required students to think only at this lowest level.

Teacher: How do you count the sixteenth notes in measure 29?

Students: Ta-ka-di-mi *(or any equivalent non-number response)*.

Teacher: Good.

The correct answer only required students to think at the lowest level of the taxonomy in which previously learned, memorized knowledge is recalled.

Students who look at the same measure and answer *3-e-&-a* are also required to search their memory banks and to recall the fact that sixteenths are counted as ... *e-&-a's* in 4/4 time. The difference is that these students must then use that stored memory as the *starting point* for some higher level thinking before they can come up with the coveted correct answer. They must apply their general knowledge of the counting of sixteenths to solve the puzzle of this particular set of sixteenths. *"Are these sixteenths 1-e-&-a, or 2-e-&-a, or 3-e-&-a, or 4-e-&-a? Let's see. The half note is the first two counts in the measure, so the sixteenths are 3-e-&-a."* Using the lowest level of recalled knowledge as a platform, the students are forced to jump to the higher level thinking skills of *comprehension, analysis, and application.*

Students who memorized in 5th grade that four sixteenth notes are counted *Ti-ri-ti-ri* never again have to do any fresh thinking in order to supply us with the correct answer to our counting questions. Even asking the question might be considered a waste of time. Research has demonstrated that students can come up with the correct answers to our counting questions by engaging in different levels of thinking. Unfortunately, in our educational culture in which the correct answer is prized above all else, many students will only employ the degree of thinking that is required to win the praise that accompanies a correct answer. There is no need for engaging a higher level of thinking. They got the right answer through simple recall. Their objective has been met. We have a responsibility to challenge our students to apply higher order thinking skills as often as possible in our teaching. In my personal view, the number- counting systems give us more opportunities to ask rhythm questions that require higher order thinking skills. Common sense also tells me that students find their educational experience to be more meaningful when they are given frequent opportunities to think at more complex levels. Thinking deeply is a pleasurable and satisfying human activity.

Putting Rhythms Into Space

The vast majority of concerts that I conducted during my thirty-year career in the public schools were with students in grades five through nine. This is not the most stable and reliable age group to stand in front of on concert nights. As many will attest, it is not for the faint of heart. Stage fright, excess adrenaline, lack of focus, and so forth can, without warning, cause young students to do any number of strange and wondrous things. They can suddenly create events that never, ever occurred in rehearsals, resulting in moments of concert chaos. I do not believe that this is what the term *chance music* really means, by the way. For the first time ever, the trombone entry may be one count early, which becomes the start of an impending train wreck. When the trombone car jumps the track, all of the cars that follow it become unstable. Most of the time the train stays on the track, but only after an interval of sheer terror. "Whew! Almost lost it. I'm so thankful that the composer put that fermata there!" Occasionally the train completely derails, and the group has to stop while the conductor quietly sets all of the cars back on the track. In a voice just loud enough for the performers to hear, he says, "Measure 127." If he is an experienced conductor, measure 127 is most likely beyond the point of the derailment. No time to fix the track now, and certainly no sense taking a chance on a replay of that disaster, right? Embarrassing.

I can honestly report that none of the above ever happened to me, which I agree could be considered a great measure of good luck. In reality, however, I attribute only a very small part of it to luck. After my first few years of teaching, the thought of the above kinds of disasters occurring during concerts truthfully never crossed my mind. In retrospect, I believe those kinds of situations were averted, mainly because of two rehearsal strategies that I consistently employed that enabled my students to be extraordinarily confident in their rhythmic performance. I feel certain that both of these strategies are more understandable and function better if students use a number-counting system. The success that resulted from these practices is the most significant reason that I recommend a number-counting system rather than a non-number system. They are strategies that I am delighted to be able to share with you in the hopes that you may find them interesting and, perhaps, useful. The first of these I refer to as *Putting Rhythms Into Space.* Literally hundreds and hundreds of times a year, my students were asked to envision their rhythms *in space.* They were encouraged to imaginatively take them off the flat piece of paper in front of them and to *see them* sitting in three dimensional space.

"... and Where is That?"

To illustrate the concept of *Putting Rhythms Into Space,* we will continue using the same rehearsal scenario as before. The students experience difficulty playing the following measure:

Teacher: How do you count the sixteenth notes in this measure?

Students: 3-e-&-a.

*An important **four-word question** invariably follows the correct answer to the counting question.*

Teacher: **And where is that?**

Students: *The student response to the question is always nonverbal. They simply point in the general direction of where count three is in a conductor's 4/4 pattern.*

Teacher: Correct. The sixteenths are right here. *He indicates the area in front of him and to his immediate right where the beat point of count three will be when he conducts. He points to that area and encourages the students to imagine the four sixteenths sitting there.*

Can you see them? There they are. Keep your eyes on them. *Students seem to enjoy the imaginative play of the visualization. He continues.*

Still pointing in the general vicinity of count three, he says: As you can see, these four notes are just sitting there. They are completely lifeless. They cannot and will not come to life and move through the air until they are touched by **the magic wand**. *At the mention of the words "the magic wand," he waves his conducting baton in the air for all to see.*

Watch! Keep your eyes on the lifeless sixteenths sitting at count three. *He conducts counts one and two as he sings the half note. He executes a slight delay at the end of count two to call extra attention to his upcoming touching of the sixteenths on count three. He conducts a somewhat emphatic count three as his and all of the students' eyes are on the imagined sixteenth notes sitting there. As he sings the sixteenths, his eyes appear to follow them as they move off into space at the touch of the baton. He finishes the measure with the quarter note.*

Teacher: Did you see that? Let me do it one more time. Watch again. Keep your eyes on the sixteenths! They can only come to life when they are touched by the baton. *The demonstration is repeated with an even bigger delay getting to count three.*

Do it with me a few times. *He indicates a pitch for all to sing along with him. Sometimes he delays the arrival to count three; other times he does not. The entire emphasis is on count three. That is where the sixteenth notes are. They are not on the paper. They are sitting in space at count three.*

Good job! Now play the rhythm several times on a concert "F." *Once again count three is sometimes delayed, sometimes early. The students become experts at executing the sixteenths precisely on beat three.*

Great! Let's play measure 29 as written now. Those of you who actually have the sixteenths in your part know exactly where they are. I expect to see your eyes on them when we get there. **They are not on your paper; they are sitting up here near me, waiting for YOU to bring them to life**. And the rest of you need to look up here also, because count three just might be a little late. Actually, it could even be early. You won't know unless you *see* when count three is touched. *As the measure is played, the teacher's eyes are on the ensemble, making sure that all eyes are on count three. The measure is played several times, the last couple with no delay to count three. The problem has been solved in an imaginative, enjoyable, engaging, important, and creative way.*

As was stated before, these types of visualization exercises were done hundreds of times a year, at every available opportunity. Consistent repetition spaced over an extended period of time is one of our most effective teaching tools. "Horns: What count is your "A" on? *And where is that?* Look up here and play it at the exact instant it is touched." In my experience, these frequent visualizations enabled the students to have a truly meaningful encounter with the rhythms under scrutiny. The students' individual visions of those rhythms scooting off into space undoubtedly left a more indelible impression on their minds than any verbal explanation involving static, black symbols on a white piece of paper ever could have. I remember one day noticing a young student looking at her rhythm in space with special intensity. On the spur of the moment I asked her what color her notes were and, without hesitation, she told me they were red. I thought, "How wonderful! Those notes are really alive for her." Visualization is a powerful and imaginative tool that we can use to bring rhythms to life for our students.

There are three important things that need to be in place in order for students to gain the most benefit from this concept of *Notes in Space*.

(1)   The emphasis of the visualization is always on *when rhythmic figures start*. Think again about the rhythm problem we have been discussing. Since the real problem has been the fact that some of the students were not playing the half note correctly, it would seem logical to zero in on the fact that the half note is two counts. Although that mistake needs to be verbally pointed out, emphasizing the *performance* of the half note would not solve the problem nearly as easily as focusing on when the sixteenth notes start. There would most likely be some students in the ensemble who would continue to play the measure incorrectly if the emphasis was on the half note. When they were reminded to be sure to give the half note two counts, they would concentrate on tapping their feet twice, but still might play the sixteenths early, on the "&" of two. They would be giving the half note two *taps*, but only one-and-a-half *counts*. On the other hand, if the students would simply focus on starting the sixteenths on count three, they wouldn't have to be concerned about how long the half note was. *The half note lasts until the sixteenths start!* The concentration needs to be on starting notes on time.

What I am about to say may seem to some to be a preposterous idea, but its truth cannot be denied. Think about it. In performing a passage of music, if every single note and rest is started on time, there is no need to be concerned about durations. They have to be correct. I am convinced that it is far easier for students to understand and execute *the beginnings of notes* than it is for them to comprehend and execute *the ends of notes*. If all of the notes are started on time, the ends of the preceding notes have to be correct. The above rhythm problem was solved completely by concentrating on when the sixteenths started, not on how long the half note lasted. I repeat. If every note is started on time, rhythm problems are virtually eliminated. Every note lasts until the next one starts. The question, *"and where is that?"* always needs to be directed to where on the conducting pattern a note or rhythmic figure sits, waiting to be started on its journey.

This principle rings true even when stylistic considerations are taken into account. For example, it might be argued that a passage consisting of *staccato* notes could not be interpreted correctly if each note lasted until the next one started. That is obviously true. However, the spaces between staccato notes are *stylistic* in nature rather than mathematical. We do not teach students that staccato quarter notes in 4/4 are 13/16ths of a count. The space between the notes is not measured. It is interpreted by conductors and modified by circumstances. In a gymnasium, staccato notes are shorter than they are in a performance venue with less reverberation, but they all start on time.

(2)   In order for the student visualizations to be completely effective, our conducting patterns must be absolutely clear and easily readable. Each beat point must have its own place in space, and all of our students must know where they are. Our beat patterns must be unambiguous.

(3)   Students who can themselves conduct will relate more meaningfully to our conducting. We need to teach our students to conduct! Not until they internalize the various conducting patterns that they will see during the year will they fully understand them. Having students conduct is another enjoyable activity that can be practiced on a frequent basis, and which requires very little extra class time. In a band situation, for example, as the brass play their warm-up scale in four-count notes, all of the woodwinds can conduct from their seats. Since we don't really need to watch the brass as they play the scale, our eyes can be on *the non-playing conductors*. We can give visual pats on the back to excellent conductors, subtly correct less than perfect patterns, and so forth. Then, as the woodwinds play the scale, the brass can become the conductors. The percussion can conduct both groups. After the pattern is thoroughly learned, of course, various students can actually advance to the podium for the warm-up, basically leading both the body of student conductors as well as the current players. This allows us to be physically in among the non-playing conductors, offering assistance where needed, praise where deserved.

I used to be concerned about the problem of the mirror effect relative to conducting. When first introducing a four pattern to the students, I turned around with my back to them so that they could copy my model exactly. Later, as my students were sitting in their seats conducting a four-beat pattern with me on the podium facing them, we all moved to our left for count two but, of course, my left now looked to be their right. My concern was unfounded. It was never a problem. I believe that the students understood the pattern so well that they realized that we were all moving down, *left,* right, and up for 1,2,3, and 4. It also helped that many of them got to spend some time on the podium during the year. Through experience, they learned that conductors don't change patterns because of the direction they are facing.

Obviously, students must become familiar with all of the various conducting patterns that they will experience. Young students should be competent in the conducting of at least the two and three-count patterns, as well as the four-pattern. We need to add conducting to the list of skills that our students will acquire right from the beginning. They come to us already skilled in verbal communication. As music teachers, it is our responsibility to teach them the non-verbal language spoken by conductors. Conducting cannot be a foreign language to our students if two-way communication is to be established. They must be able to read this unique sign language.

Having students put rhythms into space is one of two significant reasons that I consider the number based counting systems to better serve the needs of performing ensembles. A non-number system could certainly be made to work, but in my view it would not be nearly as simple and logical for the students to comprehend. Adults could adjust with relative ease, but perhaps not students.

In order for the visualizations to work most effectively, it is imperative that students quickly recognize each rhythmic element's numerical place in a measure of music. This is not a skill reserved for only the most experienced musicians. Very young students can learn to do it as well. Almost without conscious thought, students who are "brought up" using a number counting system like the one described here will recognize that the eighth notes in a particular 4/4 measure are on count two. That is because they have always called such notes *"2-&."* Students who use a non-number system have always called the same notes *"du-de,"* or *"ti-ti,"* and the like. Knowing that they are on count two is not as "automatic" for them as it is for students who have always called them *"2-&."* Extra time and thought is required, but it is necessary if the students are to coordinate the notes with the conductor's beat two. Unfortunately, in performance situations, there is often not time for them to translate their well-known *"ti-ti"* into a *"2-&."* They can learn to do it, but in my view, not especially easily or quickly. I am convinced that it is more logical, natural, and simple for students who have grown up calling the two eighth notes *"2-&"* to instantly recognize that they are on count two and to be able to coordinate that with the baton's count two.

A Controversial Idea on Cueing

It was stated earlier that I had the extreme good fortune of never having to be concerned about the possibility of my groups falling apart during a performance. A great deal of the credit for that goes to the fact that my students consistently, all year long, were challenged to coordinate their printed rhythms with the corresponding beat locations of the baton. They knew how to put rhythms into space. Based on their ability to successfully make those critical connections, a second closely related strategy was practiced throughout the year. It is an idea that tends to go against the grain of traditional conducting practice, but it is one that I feel is worth hearing. Once again, I offer this only for the intellectual challenge and curiosity that it embodies. It is not my intention to attempt to change or interfere with any success that you are enjoying in the area of giving cues from the podium. I offer it merely as food for thought.

In my thirty years of conducting rehearsals and concerts, I can honestly say that **I never gave a cue**. As a matter of fact, if you were to guest conduct any of my ensembles, and if you told the trombones, "I'll cue you," no one in the group would have any idea what you were talking about. "Cue" was not a part of our class vocabulary.

Beginning early in the year and consistently reinforced throughout the year, all of my students heard various versions of the following lecture:

> "I will never, ever look at you and tell you when to play. *That is your job, not mine*. I have far too much on my mind to have to remember that you are supposed to come in on count two after four measures of rest. You have all of the skills and knowledge you need to be able to do that for yourselves. You certainly don't need my help to accomplish such a simple task. I repeat; knowing when to play is your job, not mine! I cannot and will not do it for you. During the four measures of rest, you will watch my conducting pattern as intently as you would if you were playing. Every time the baton comes straight down, it signals the start of another measure of rest. Watching me all the way, you will count your part like this, coordinating every single count with the down, left, right, up of my conducting." While he demonstrates counting the four measures of rest aloud, he calls student attention to the baton.

> **Counting four measures plus one count of rest in 4/4**
> Students coordinate all counts with conductor's baton.
> *1*-2-3-4
> *2*-2-3-4
> *3*-2-3-4
> *4*-2-3-4
> *1*-*PLAY!*

"It is your responsibility to come in confidently when the baton is on count two in that fifth measure, whether I am looking at you or not.

However, it could very well be that every time we rehearse that part, I actually am looking directly at you. You must understand that if that happens, I am telling you *how* to play, not *when* to play. I am letting you know that you have the most important thing in the piece right now. You are in the spotlight! By the way I conduct, I am reminding you that the part needs to be played sweetly or aggressively, or whatever. Just remember, though, it is your job to be there on count two. And, of course, you know where that is. It's right here (pointing to the area of the conducting pattern where count two occurs). And you need to understand one final thing. Even if I look at you at that spot during every single rehearsal, I might not during the concert. At that moment in the concert, my attention might be needed somewhere else. I might be trying to signal the flute soloist to raise the pitch, or to quiet the saxophones down, or whatever. Don't ever depend on me to tell you when to play! Be there!"

I am convinced that this highly unusual practice is the second major reason that the students were always where they needed to be without my having to worry about them. It was made abundantly clear to them over and over throughout the year that they needed to be self-reliant, and they responded admirably to the challenge. They never once let us down.

I have witnessed countless rehearsals during which the group is stopped, the conductor picks up a pencil and marks the score while saying, "Clarinets, I'll cue you right there." What has just happened? The conductor has taken on yet another job. He must now remember to tell the clarinets when to play. If he forgets to cue the clarinets during the concert, there could be real problems. The students no longer have to think about the four measures plus one count of rest. Through the experience of countless rehearsals, they have learned to come in when pointed at. Even if they diligently count their rests during the concert, some will doubt that they counted accurately if they don't get the all-important "go-ahead" from the podium. That's what they were trained to look for. No thinking required. On more than one occasion I have heard students answer their conductor's post-concert question concerning what went wrong with, "You didn't cue us."

I am personally convinced that when we tell our students that we will cue them, many of them get the following, completely unintended message: "He thinks I'm too stupid to be able to figure out when to play! Well, fine. I'll just let him do my thinking for me." Our students are perfectly capable of thinking for themselves. As a matter of fact, when told that it is 100% their responsibility to always be at the right place at the right time, their self-esteem and sense of pride is significantly enhanced. They will be there! Young people want responsibility. They want to be independent, to think for themselves. Any group in which all of the members are given important responsibilities will be a more dynamic group than one in which the leader does most of the thinking and the members become mere followers.

Of course, none of this works unless the students are really tied to the baton and have a thorough understanding of its many functions. Among others, the baton is *the road map* that students can check at any point during the trip to make sure they are in the right place. Students need to know that the downbeat is the start of every measure in the piece. At every opportunity during rehearsals, students need to practice seeing important rhythmic figures sitting at the appropriate places on their director's conducting patterns, and they need to be given the responsibility for always getting themselves where they need to be. They will not disappoint if given abundant, daily opportunities to practice this skill. And they will be more inclined to spend time watching their conductor, something that many young musicians don't do very well.

In retrospect, I suppose I actually did give abundant cues. It's just that my definition of the word "cue" was probably different than many. My cues were not telling students *when* to play. They were telling them *how* to play. My students knew that it was their responsibility to be there, but experience probably told them that I would most likely meet them there, so that I could help them to play the passage as musically as possible. The success of this strategy gave me the freedom to concentrate completely on the MUSIC, not on the mechanics of keeping the train on the track.

Final Thoughts on Counting Systems in Simple Meter

For the reasons that I hope I have been able to make clear, it is my personal belief that any of the *numbered* counting system is better suited to performance ensembles than any of the non-number systems. Much of the literature experienced by performers in instrumental groups in particular demands a considerable degree of independence on the parts of students. Very often students playing the same instruments have rhythmically dissimilar parts. First, second, and third clarinet parts, for example, are often written with simultaneously different rhythms in each of the three parts. All students in performance groups must be able to determine, on their own, where they are in the music at all times.

The key to helping students maintain their rhythmic independence amid the confusion of divergent parts lies in the conductor's baton. Students who understand their conductor's beat patterns can always know whether or not they are in the right place. If they should become temporarily lost, they know that they simply need to start the next measure on the following *beat one -* the next downbeat. They don't have to sit there and wonder "Where are we?" The baton informs them, "We're starting the next measure. Join us again." It goes without saying that students must have their attention drawn to the baton at every rehearsal. This process of coordinating written rhythms with baton locations is a skill that demands unrelenting emphasis, but which pays huge dividends. Students who are consistently invited to *put rhythmic figures into space* and who know that it is always their responsibility to *cue themselves* and know when to come in, will develop the required self-reliance that their music demands. Students who associate the *numbers* of a rhythm's *lyrics* with their conductor's corresponding *numbered beat locations* stand the best chance of achieving rhythmic independence.

Part Four

Teaching Compound Meter

The Two Meters: Simple and Compound

As we start to look at compound meter, it is important that we are thinking of the musical terms *simple* and *compound* in the same way. I do not believe that meter, simple or compound, is determined by notation or time signature. Notation and time signature simply demonstrate how the composer chose to symbolize what he or she was trying to express. Meter is determined by *how the music sounds*. To my way of thinking, the ear determines meter first, then the eyes confirm it. Specifically, it is **how the one-beat sound is divided**. The one-beat sound is defined as the pulse to which the conductor moves his baton or the listener taps his foot, regardless of the notation. When listening to music, if the one-beat sound is consistently divided into two equal parts, the music is in simple meter. To this point in the book, we have been discussing only simple meter. If the one-beat sound is consistently divided into three equal parts, the music is compound. It is the division of the one-beat sound that determines meter.

If I were to sing a short, improvised melody for you that had two beats to the measure, and if the tune consisted entirely of one-count and two-count sounds, as you listened you could not possibly know if it was in simple or compound meter. You would be unable to determine if I had been thinking:

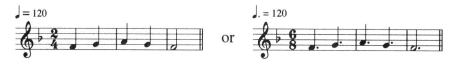

Not until I divided one or more of the beats could meter be surmised.

Simple Meter: The one-beat sounds are divided into two equal parts.

Compound Meter: The one-beat sounds are divided into three equal parts.

Simple Meter

When the one-beat sounds are divided into *two equal parts*, the music is in **simple meter**. Think of it as *simple* cell division. Each individual cell splits into two equal parts throughout the entire structure in simple meters.

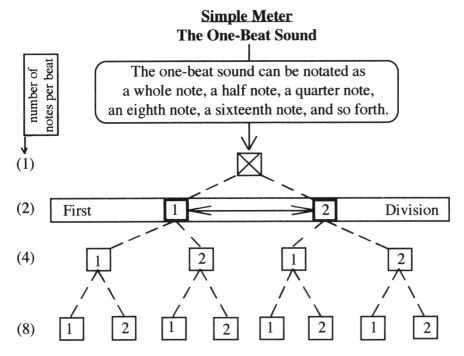

Simple Meter
The One-Beat Sound

number of notes per beat

The one-beat sound can be notated as a whole note, a half note, a quarter note, an eighth note, a sixteenth note, and so forth.

(1)

(2) First — 1 ⟷ 2 — Division

(4)

(8)

On the occasion that any single cell in simple meter splits into three equal parts, *it is an exception* and must be labeled with the number *"3"* printed above or below the three notes. This triple division of a single cell is called a "triplet."

Compound Meter

When the one-beat sounds are consistently divided into *three equal parts*, the music is in **compound meter**. The splitting in compound meter is not the same throughout the entire structure as it is in simple meter. In simple meter, each and every individual cell naturally splits into two equal parts. Any cell that splits into three equal parts is an exception and must be labeled like the cell pictured above. In compound meter, the one-beat sound *naturally splits into three equal parts* and, therefore, does not need to be labeled when it is written. It is not an exception. Three is the natural division of the one-beat sound. Other than this splitting of the one-beat sound into three parts, however, all other cells in the entire structure of compound meter split into only two parts, as in simple meter. Any of those cells that split into three must also be labeled as triplets.

Compound Meter
The One-Beat Sound

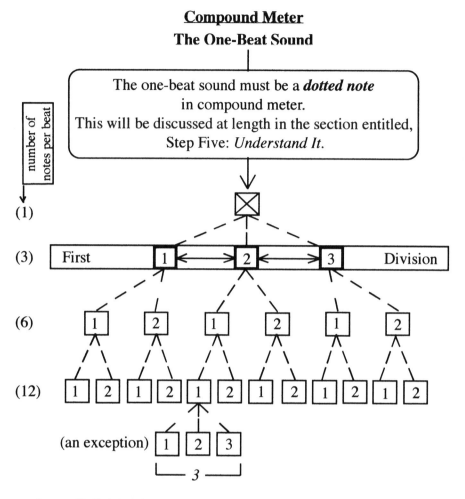

Any cell division in compound meter that does not conform to the above diagram is an exception and must be labeled as such. If the first division of the one-beat sound is into only two equal parts rather than the normal three, that exception will be labeled with a *"2"* and called a "duplet." Duplets are not seen as often as triplets.

The Duplet in Compound Meter
The One-Beat Sound

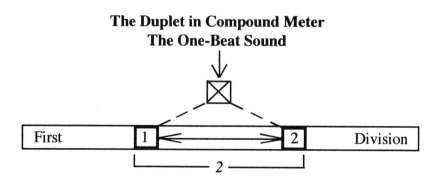

> ## "Teaching 6/8 in six is teaching music unmusically!"

What a harsh statement! Who would say such a thing? To whom? And why? I said it. To myself. Because I couldn't stop that thought from entering my mind. I didn't like it, but I couldn't escape it. Near the beginning of my career, as my band students finished up a unit of study in 6/8, I had the same, haunting thought that is expressed above. We had finally gotten through all the etudes and exercises intended to introduce and teach 6/8. Now came the reward -- actual songs. But something was terribly wrong. As the students clunked their way through songs like "Three Blind Mice," "The Farmer in the Dell," "Row, Row, Row Your Boat," "Pop! Goes the Weasel," and the like -- played six beats to the measure -- I had to admit it. I had taught music unmusically. Those songs *had* to be performed two beats to the measure. The students were playing everything *correctly*, but it wasn't musical. In order for them to achieve the wonderful musical lilt and sway that the songs demanded, I realized that the students should not be concentrating on each individual eighth note as I had taught them to do. Compare the readings of two different versions of the lyrics to one well-known, often used 6/8 song below: (UPPER CASE equals emphasis)

OV-ER THE RI-VER AND THROUGH-OUGH THE WO-ODS,
TO GRAND-MOTH-ER'S HOU-OUSE WE GO-O-O-O-O....
or
OV-er the RI-ver and THROUGH the WOODS,
to GRAND-moth-er's HOUSE we GO....

Why were my students basically emphasizing every single syllable, the important as well as the unimportant, in the familiar 6/8 songs that they were playing? Because I had taught them to give every eighth note one count instead of one-third of a count as the *music* demanded. In order to be musical, the songs required that the students feel the eighth notes in groups of three. I should have introduced them to compound 6/8, two beats to the measure, from the very beginning. But I didn't know how.

Why did I introduce 6/8 in six? Because it made logical sense. We started the new unit with something they knew, allowing the students to go *from the known to the unknown*, which is a sound educational principle. What they knew, of course, was that the bottom number of the time signature informed them that eighth notes get one count. If eighth notes get one count, then quarter notes have to get two, and blah, blah, blah. They were not at all happy about any of this, as they dearly loved their one-count quarter notes, but they persevered and finally got to the songs which, it turns out, sounded really dumb. Because they were familiar songs, the students knew that they didn't sound right, but they didn't say anything. Let's face it. They just wanted to finish the unit. They didn't like 6/8 at all, and if these songs were what 6/8 was all about, they had good reason not to like it. All that work, only to arrive at such an unmusical destination. No wonder they moaned and groaned every time they saw new music in 6/8.

I tried to fix the problem by having the students play the songs faster, while still counting and tapping in six. Then I asked them to play the songs, which by now they could play very well, at the same brisk tempo, but to tap only on counts one and four, thereby grouping the eighth notes into threes. Once they could do that, I explained that count one could still be called "1," but count four was now count *"2,"* the start of the *"2nd"* group of three eighth notes. About that time I would begin to notice that certain look on their faces. You know the one I mean. The one that I was sure was saying, "Ya' know Mr. Newell, you aren't making any sense at all." Of course I explained very scientifically and logically why all of this had to be, but they were basically having none of it. The harm had already been done. They had been introduced to 6/8 as a heavy-handed, clunk-a-long, one-eighth-note-at-a-time kind of thing, and they just couldn't seem to relax and get the natural swing of it. I truly believe that there is a significant amount of truth to the old saying, "First impressions are lasting impressions." So far as 6/8 was concerned, I had damaged them.

Teaching Compound 6/8

Introducing students to 6/8, two beats to the measure from the very beginning, is extremely easy and enjoyable for both students and teachers. Teachers don't actually have to *teach it*, because students can already *do it*.

THE RHYTHM LEARNING SEQUENCE
Step One
The Musical Magic of Mother Goose

******

Mr. Johnston: This morning we are going to start working with a new rhythm sound. I am going to chant something that I am certain all of you know very well. As soon as you recognize what I'm saying, I want you to join me. See if you can be the first person in your row to join in. *He starts a gentle lap pat at about 84 beats per minute, which the students imitate. All the students join the chant shortly after hearing the first two words.*

Without stopping he goes on immediately to other nursery rhymes that are obviously in compound meter. The students continue to join him after hearing just the first words.

Teacher: Terrific! See, I told you you'd know what I was chanting. Now, I want you to pick up your instruments and play "Jack and Jill" up the Bb Scale. Just think of the words as you play. It'll go like this. *So that they understand when to change pitches, he sings it for them while patting the beat.*

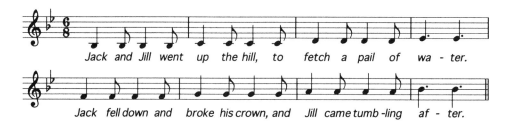

Sing it with me one time, and then we'll play it.

******

The students first sing it and then play it perfectly. They have no idea that they are doing something that is generally considered to be rather difficult. They are simply having a good time recalling nursery rhymes from their childhood. It is interesting to note that, because they are performing the nursery rhymes on scales, they are learning that there are two beats to a measure in compound 6/8. It has not been explained to them, and it won't be for quite a while. They are just doing it. It is becoming a part of their instrumental rhythmic repertoire.

This warm-up procedure involving Step One: *Perform It* continues for the next several classes. Sometimes nursery rhymes are reviewed from previous days. Other times new ones are introduced. They are chanted first, then played. The students are encouraged to be thinking the lyrics as they play the scale. Snare drummers play the lyrics of the nursery rhyme along with all of the winds. Proper 6/8 snare sticking is taught and monitored by the teacher. The bass drummer plays the two, even beats per measure, helping everyone to feel the basic rhythmic structure of "6/8 in 2."

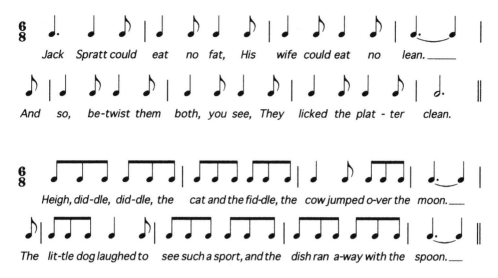

To prolong their work with the sounds and performance of compound meter, Mr. Johnston teaches the students a few nursery rhymes that are less well-known. He teaches them the rhymes one phrase at a time, by rote. The more the students practice these "sounds of childhood," the easier it will be for them to later associate the sounds with notation. It goes without saying that he carefully chooses only nursery rhymes that are clearly in compound meter. On nursery rhymes like the one below, the initial eighth note pickup is played on the concert Bb. And since the students always change pitches on count one when doing rhythmic scale exercises, the pickup note to the second lines on this page are still played on the fourth scale degree.

Students who have done any baby-sitting relate especially well to this amusing and likely unfamiliar nursery rhyme. It starts with the eighth note pickup, a very common rhythmic figure in compound 6/8 meter. The teacher "counts them off" in compound meter to help them chant and play the pickup note accurately.

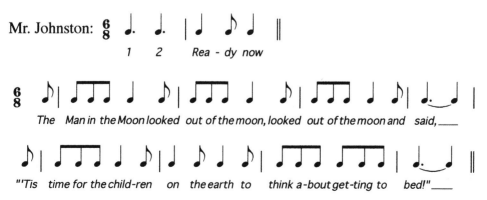

As his students recall the lyrics to various nursery rhymes and, through them, transfer the sound and feel of compound meter to their instruments, their teacher sometimes has them play different nursery rhymes at the same time as duets. One example follows:

At other times the teacher has the woodwinds go up the scale as the brass come down, with both groups playing either the same or different nursery rhymes. Occasionally he has one student play a "mystery" nursery rhyme, with the others having to guess its name, just from the rhythmic sounds the soloist makes. Since many nursery rhymes have similar rhythmic schemes, there are multiple wrong guesses, a "game" that the students enjoy.

During the reciting and performance of these nursery rhymes, no explanation of compound meter is offered. The performances are perfect. They are being done flawlessly and effortlessly. The students have a natural feel for compound 6/8. They don't need any of our words of wisdom at this time. They are simply laying the groundwork that will enable them to associate these things they can already do with the corresponding notation when the time comes.

The Rhythm of Childhood

I have long called compound meter *the rhythm of childhood*. Envision a child skipping down a sidewalk. What do you see and hear?

When young children skip, their whole bodies are performing in compound meter. Combining that with nursery rhymes gives students years of valuable experience with compound meter before we ever see them in our classes. We do not have to teach children to do compound meter! We simply have to harvest their experience.

How was I teaching 6/8 before I discovered the magic of *Mother Goose* and *The Rhythm Learning Sequence*? First of all, by violating the principles of the sequence. Instead of having them *perform* the sounds first, I began by *telling* them what I thought they needed to know. Each year as I was explaining simple 6/8 in six to them, I distinctly remember thinking, "I hope that someday these kids can pick up their instruments and play 'The Washington Post March' or '76 Trombones' and the like, in a perfectly wonderful, lilting compound 6/8. I really don't know how they're going to get there from here, but I hope they do." If the students could have read my mind, they very well might have interrupted all my meaningless, boring, non-productive, unmusical talk with something like:

"Mr. Newell, Mr. Newell,

We can already do what you want!

I was teaching exclusively to my students' analytical left brains, talking about the meanings of the numbers in time signatures, mathematical ratios, comparing new note durations to their tried and true 4/4, and the like. And all the while, residing in their right brains was a wealth of experience with compound meter. I didn't realize that they had that resource sitting there to draw upon, and they didn't know what I was hoping they would someday be able to do. Talk about two ships passing in the night!

Important, Related Activity

At the same time that the students are working on the natural sound and feel of compound meter through nursery rhymes, a related activity needs to take place in the classroom. Students need to be made aware of the different look of one, two, three, and four-count notes in compound meter. Since one, two, three, and four-count notes are not *new sounds* for students, the instruction can begin at Step Three of *The Rhythm Learning Sequence,* "See It." This new material is presented as separate, short segments during warm-up routines.

******

Mr. Johnston: Let's begin our warm-up today to this rhythm. *He walks to the chalkboard and writes the following:*

$$\frac{4}{4} \quad \textbf{o} \qquad |$$

The students play the Bb Major Scale, four counts per pitch. Upon completion of the playing of the scale, he adds a measure to the one already on the board, after which he provides some necessary explanation.

$$\frac{4}{4} \quad \textbf{o} \qquad | \frac{12}{8} \quad \textbf{o.} \qquad |$$

First of all, I need to tell you that you are to **ignore the time signature** in this new measure. Don't even try to figure out what the numbers mean, because they don't mean what you think. This is something totally new and different. As a matter of fact, over the next several classes, whenever I write a time signature on the board that has the number "8" on the bottom, just ignore it. You will understand it all when you need to. You just have to trust me on this. You do trust me, don't you? *This question brings the expected laughter.*

All you need to know at this time is that this note in the second measure is a very close relative of the note in the first measure. **They are both whole notes, and they both get four counts.** The only difference between them is that the whole note in the 12/8 measure is dotted. Let's play the scale again, but now to both measures. Keep your eyes on the chalkboard.

As they perform the scale, playing the four-count Bb in 4/4, the four-count C in compound 12/8, and so forth, the teacher points to each note as it is played.

Mr. Johnston: Good. Now, let's add a third measure. *He adds the following:*

$$\frac{4}{4}\ \mathbf{o}\ \bigg|\ \frac{12}{8}\ \mathbf{o\cdot}\ \bigg|\ \frac{4}{4}\ \text{\musicalnote}\ \text{\musicalnote}\ \bigg|$$

Nothing new here. Ready, play. *The students play the three measures of rhythm up the one octave Concert Bb Scale, repeating back to the first measure until they reach the octave Bb. The scale ends on the 12/8 measure.*

Now watch. Something new is coming. *Mr. Johnston adds another measure to the three already on the chalkboard.*

$$\frac{4}{4}\ \mathbf{o}\ \bigg|\ \frac{12}{8}\ \mathbf{o\cdot}\ \bigg|\ \frac{4}{4}\ \text{\musicalnote}\ \text{\musicalnote}\ \bigg|\ \frac{12}{8}\ \text{\musicalnote}\ \text{\musicalnote}\ \bigg|$$

I need to tell you something about this last measure. It is incorrect. What I wanted was for it to sound exactly like the measure before it, but right now it won't. I have to change it slightly. Does anyone want to guess what I have to do to the half notes in this last measure to make them sound exactly like the half notes in the 4/4 measure?

Rebecca: Add dots?

Mr. Johnston; Exactly! Terrific, Rebecca. There's a pattern here, no? *He changes the half notes in the 12/8 measure to dotted half notes, and the students play the entire four measures up the scale. Mr. Johnston points to each measure as it is played.*

$$*\ \frac{4}{4}\ \mathbf{o}\ \bigg|\ \frac{12}{8}\ \mathbf{o\cdot}\ \bigg|\ \frac{4}{4}\ \text{\musicalnote}\ \text{\musicalnote}\ \bigg|\ \frac{12}{8}\ \text{\musicalnote\cdot}\ \text{\musicalnote\cdot}\ \bigg|$$

> * There is absolutely no reason to add the indication that ♩=♩. anywhere in these kinds of exercises. It would be totally meaningless to the students and is unnecessary at this time. It is clearly an important concept to be covered at an appropriate time in the future, but not now.

Mr. Johnston: Good job. Pretty easy stuff, no? Let's add another measure. *He walks to the chalkboard and adds a measure of quarter notes in 4/4.*

Any questions? Good. Let's play again from the beginning. *As each measure is played, he continues pointing to that measure.*

$$\frac{4}{4} \; \mathbf{o} \; \Big| \frac{12}{8} \; \mathbf{o}. \; \Big| \frac{4}{4} \; \downarrow \; \downarrow \; \Big| \frac{12}{8} \; \downarrow. \; \downarrow. \; \Big| \frac{4}{4} \; \downarrow \downarrow \downarrow \downarrow \Big|$$

Mr. Johnston: I'm going to add one final measure for today. I think some of you know what I'm going to do already. *He moves to the chalkboard and adds the final measure.*

$$\frac{4}{4} \; \mathbf{o} \; \Big| \frac{12}{8} \; \mathbf{o}. \; \Big| \frac{4}{4} \; \downarrow \; \downarrow \; \Big| \frac{12}{8} \; \downarrow. \; \downarrow. \; \Big| \frac{4}{4} \; \downarrow \downarrow \downarrow \downarrow \Big| \frac{12}{8} \; \downarrow \downarrow \downarrow \downarrow \Big|$$

As he turns around to face the students, fully one-half of them are waving their arms in the air. They seem very anxious to be called upon. Someone needs to help this teacher out!

James: If you want those last four notes to be one count each, you're going to have to add dots to them.

Mr. Johnston; You're absolutely right! I guess I forgot again. Thank you, James. *He corrects the measure, and the students play the exercise in its entirety, up the scale, ending on the 12/8 dotted whole note.*

$$\frac{4}{4} \; \mathbf{o} \; \Big| \frac{12}{8} \; \mathbf{o}. \; \Big| \frac{4}{4} \; \downarrow \; \downarrow \; \Big| \frac{12}{8} \; \downarrow. \; \downarrow. \; \Big| \frac{4}{4} \; \downarrow \downarrow \downarrow \downarrow \Big| \frac{12}{8} \; \downarrow. \; \downarrow. \; \downarrow. \; \downarrow. \Big|$$

The learning that has taken place during this short warm-up lesson has been intentionally *active* rather than *passive*. It is the students who have been telling the teacher that two-count notes in 12/8 are *dotted* half notes and that one-count notes in 12/8 are *dotted* quarter notes. There is no doubt that they will remember this material far better than they would had the information been delivered to them in the form of a teacher lecture.

Mr. Johnston: So, before we move on, let's discuss what we've learned in the last few minutes.

Jason: That when you write 12/8 as a time signature, we are supposed to ignore it.

Mr. Johnston: Correct. Not only that, Jason, but when I write *any* time signature with an "8" on the bottom over the next few lessons, you are **not** to try to figure out what the numbers mean. Just say to yourself, "Oh, yeah. This is that new stuff." Anything else?

David: In 12/8, the notes get the same number of counts as they get in 4/4, except they are dotted.

Mr. Johnston: Right. There are lots of dots in time signatures with an "8" on the bottom, and so far they don't make much difference, do they?

******

For the next several classes, the same material is reviewed for a very short time at the beginning of every warm-up period. The rhythms are written in mixed time signatures on the chalkboard, and the students perform them perfectly. The only new material that is added during this period of time is the fact that a three-count note in 12/8 or 9/8 has to be a tied dotted half and dotted quarter. The students learn that there is no single note symbol in these new time signatures that represents a three-count sound.

The teacher does not move on until he is certain that the students are secure with these "new looks" for one, two, three, and four count notes in 6/8, 9/8, and 12/8 time. The students know that these changes are caused by that "8" on the bottom of the time signature, and that is all they need to know for now. By the end of these related studies, the students easily play, without explanation, eight-measure board rhythms like the following:

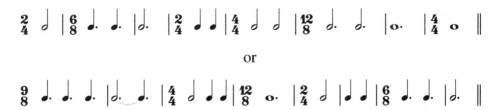

or

In an effort to make the material less exercise-like and more musical, Mr. Johnston uses his skills with notation software to write familiar, unison melodies for the students to play. These songs help students to cement into long term memory the fact that one, two, three, and four-count sounds in compound meter are written as dotted notes. This is an important concept that is learned very easily. The simple song below helps students to compare the different looks of one and two count sounds in simple and compound meters.

THE RHYTHM LEARNING SEQUENCE
Step Two
Count It

It should not be surprising that the process for helping students to learn to read compound notation is precisely the same as it is for simple meters. Before they are shown what triple division sounds look like, they need to associate their teachers' counting names to these new sounds. Since the process for doing this is covered in detail on pages 19-23, it will be presented here in abbreviated form. Because he is preparing his students for their introduction to 6/8 notation, the emphasis is switched to that time signature.

Like the counting systems that deal with simple meter, the systems in use for compound also vary widely. The triple division of the one-count sound is variously taught as *Trip-o-let, 1-la-li, Du-da-di, 1-trip-let,* plus others. A more detailed discussion of counting in compound meter will follow shortly. For illustration purposes here, we will use Mr. Johnston's preferred system, as follows:

The teacher does the familiar *My Turn, Your Turn* routine, having the students echo the now familiar "nursery rhyme rhythms" using neutral syllables. His patterns are always four beats in duration which, when eventually notated, will be shown as two measures of 6/8. As with the patterns that were used in simple meters, each pattern here also ends with a sound of at least one-count's duration.

******

Mr. Johnston; My turn, your turn, Echo me exactly. *He monitors the students' responses and insists that they also echo his musical inflections, in which he consistently puts a subtle crescendo to the start of the second measure, followed by a matching decrescendo. The students chant the rhythm patterns with a lap pat and play them with a foot tap.*

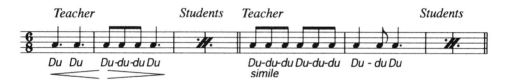

The students do this so effortlessly that the teacher moves quickly to the introduction of his preferred compound meter "lyrics." He chants a rhythmic pattern first in neutral syllables, followed immediately with the same rhythm with his preferred counting vocabulary.

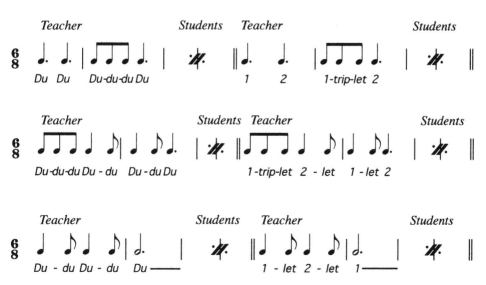

When this activity has been mastered, it is followed by the most important aspect of Step Two. The teacher presents the rhythm on neutral syllables, and the students respond immediately in counting words.

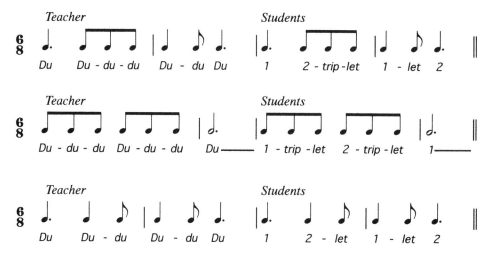

When the above kinds of exercises are being performed effortlessly and confidently by the students, it is time for them to see for the first time the musical symbols that represent the rhythms they have been saying. Since their recent warm-ups have taught them that one and two-count sounds are dotted quarters and dotted halves respectively when the bottom number of the time signature is an "8," they can focus exclusively on one thing -- what the triple division notes look like. It is time for Step Three.

THE RHYTHM LEARNING SEQUENCE
Step Three
See It

Step Three, which reveals "the look" of something they can already do, is best accomplished with flashcards. See pages 24-35 for a more comprehensive discussion of this activity.

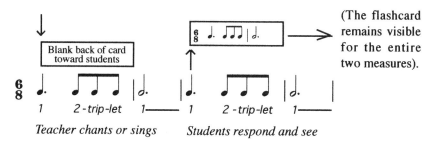

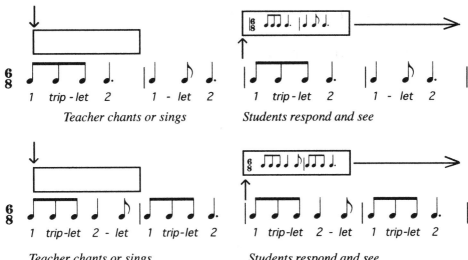

Teacher chants or sings   Students respond and see

Teacher chants or sings   Students respond and see

The above material is learned very quickly, because the only new thing for students to concentrate on is the look of the triplet eighth notes and the quarter note, eighth note combination.

The final teaching activity before moving to the actual reading of some printed music in 6/8 involves putting the "flash" in flashcards. For a more thorough look at this activity, see pages 30-32 in the simple meter part of the book. One important difference between the simple and the compound versions of this activity should be noted. When he was showing his students simple meter flashcards, Mr. Johnston "counted them off" in simple meter sounds.

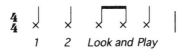

When doing this activity with compound meter flashcards, he changes his chant to reflect the sound of the meter.

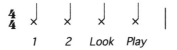

Eventually, when the students have advanced to the point that a simple meter flashcard can be followed immediately by a compound meter one, and visa versa, the chant is changed again so that neither meter is suggested.

******

Mr. Johnston: Today we get to see how fast you are. Don't take your eyes off me. You might miss it. Play the entire rhythm you see on a concert "F." Remember, we never change pitches in the middle of a flashcard. Ready?

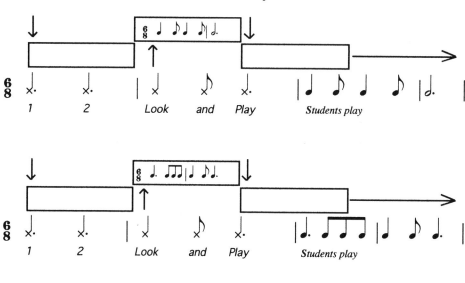

******

When the students are performing the above kinds of exercises with complete confidence, they can be pushed to excel by raising the flashcards on the word *"and."* This gives them an extremely short time to read the entire two measures. You will not know how well they can do this until you try it. As with the same type of exercises in simple meter, the students can be instructed to play or sing the compound rhythms up the scale instead of on just one pitch. Eventually the flashcards can be changed while the students are progressing up the scale. A new flashcard needs to be raised on the third beat of the rhythm currently being performed (the first beat of the second 6/8 measure). As the students play the first beat of any flashcard, we can simply be thinking to ourselves, *"1, 2, **Look, and Play.**"* Always raising a new flashcard when we hear ourselves say "look" or "and" guarantees that the students have the time required to start the new rhythm on the next scale degree. Lowering it on the word "play," guarantees that the students have to grasp the entire rhythm in an instant.

As was stated before, this flashcard activity is hugely beneficial. It forces students to see rhythms as rhythmic phrases rather than as single notes. And students enjoy it. It doesn't get much better than that.

THE RHYTHM LEARNING SEQUENCE
Step Four
Test It

It was rather boldly stated near the beginning of this *Compound Meter* section of the book that "teaching 6/8 in six is teaching music *unmusically*." Obviously, that is not always true. If the music that students are asked to perform as a result of their introduction to 6/8 is music that, in fact, was intended to be played or sung in six, then teaching 6/8 in six would be teaching music *musically*. The reason for my original negative statement is the fact that a significant amount of the 6/8 music that students will see as they go through our music programs must be performed "in two" in order to be musical. When we introduce 6/8 in six, it seems to me that we are preparing our students for *musical* failure much of the time, even though their performances will be *mathematically* correct.

This problem is especially noticeable when we first introduce the concept of 6/8 to students. A preponderance of the songs and pieces that we have them perform during that time cannot be performed musically in six. Students who go through the process in this manner have a very unsatisfactory first impression of 6/8 time. No matter how hard they work, the results are unmusical. It doesn't have to be that way.

Those of you who have read this book from the beginning realize that it is entirely possible that students can approach the reading of 6/8 notation and have no *musical* difficulties whatsoever, regardless of whether the music is in six or in two. If some of it is in simple meter, what many would call "slow 6/8," the students could very well have been doing that for a long time. Their teachers would have often had them playing and singing music in which eighth notes were one count, quarter notes were two counts, dotted-quarters were three, and so forth. Playing or singing 6/8 in six would present them with absolutely nothing new. They could musically perform, at sight and without confusion, any 6/8 music that was intended to be in six. We would simply need to tell them that for this music, they should *not* ignore the bottom number of the time signature. It actually does mean that whole notes are eight counts or that eighth notes are one, depending on which definition of the bottom number they are using at the time. We are simply going to need to help them figure out on their own when the 6/8 they see in their music is slow 6/8 (simple meter) and when it is fast 6/8 (compound meter). This is one of the many aspects of compound meter to be discussed in the next section of the book, entitled *Understand It*.

At this point in *The Rhythm Learning Sequence,* Mr. Johnston's students are ready to turn to the page in their lesson books that introduces 6/8 time. Chances are good that the songs in the unit will be ones that must be played in compound meter in order to sound "right." If the pre-book teaching of compound 6/8 has been successful, they will be able to sight-read the unit without difficulty. The students will enjoy playing both the etudes and the songs. Experience has shown that, on those occasions when classes end a lesson with a couple of extra minutes and we "take requests" for any familiar songs they want to play, very often what they want to play is the compound meter songs. To the students' ears, those songs have a happier, lighter, more carefree sound than do many of the simple meter songs. Students like 6/8 in two beats to the measure. It is fun to sing and to play.

One final point should be made. As students turn to the new unit in some instructional books, they may see that counting words have been printed under the notes. If the counting in the book spells out *1-2-3-4-5-6* for an etude or a song that must be *"in 2"* in order to be musical, the students can simply be told to ignore the written counts. I have always found students to be rather adept at ignoring things, and occasionally that is a good thing. There is certainly no reason to change books because the book suggests a certain counting. Remember, books don't teach; teachers do. The counting in the book may very well seem to be suggesting that we introduce 6/8 in six, but that is a decision for us to make. Students can simply be told that, "there is more than one way to learn 6/8, and we are learning it a different way than your book suggests. Your book is not wrong. We are just doing things differently." The students will think nothing more of it.

THE RHYTHM LEARNING SEQUENCE
Step Five
Understand It

It's unfortunate, but compound notation is probably not as easy for students to understand as is notation in simple meters. There is good reason for that. Our notation system was not designed to accommodate compound meter. However, even though understanding compound notation may not be as easy, some of the difficulty is eased by the fact that reading rhythmic notation is not, in and of itself, a new skill for students. Before they are confronted with the task of learning to read and understand compound meter, the students have extensive experience with simple meter. They understand the basic workings of rhythmic notation. As a matter of fact, as they compare the two meters, the things that they know from simple meter will very often help them to understand compound meter. And since notation in simple meter is always learned first, when confronted with compound meter, the students are older and more mature thinkers.

Our system of rhythmic notation is absolutely based on the simple mathematical principle of *division by twos*. We start with the whole note and proceed logically to the half note, followed by the quarter, the eighth, the sixteenth, the thirty-second, the sixty-fourth, the one-hundred-twenty-eighth, and so on. The system obviously works extremely well for music whose beats are divided in the same fashion -- first into two equal parts, then four, then eight, then sixteen, and so forth. It certainly should work well. It was expressly designed to represent precisely those kinds of sounds. But there is a huge body of music whose beats are not divided into halves and quarters and eighths. This music, which we have termed *compound*, has beats that are divided into thirds and sixths and twelfths, and so forth. Can these two diverse musics be represented by one system of notation, one designed to express division by twos? That is the question. How do we notate music whose beats are divided into thirds and sixths if we have to use a system designed to represent sounds divided into halves and quarters?

The answers to these and other questions are certainly not intended to be known by students in one year. Nor is it intended that they should be discussed in the order presented on the following pages. Student age, musical maturity, theoretical curiosity, teacher preferences, and the like are the best indicators of when these topics should be approached and in what order. Some are appropriate for elementary school, others for high school and beyond. In all cases, of course, mastery must ultimately be achieved if the students are to be considered literate so far as compound meter is concerned.

Compound Meter Notation Is Unnecessary

After students are competent in the performance of triplets in both simple and compound meters, they need to know why music theorists of centuries past "invented" compound meter notation. Was it really necessary? It is an indisputable fact that there has never been, and there never will be, a piece of music notated in compound 6/8, for example, that cannot be written in the more common 2/4 time signature. The following two examples of the same short melodic etude, if performed by a professional musician, would sound absolutely the same in every detail.

They sound the same, but they certainly *look different* and that, simply stated, is the reason for the existence of compound meter notation. Students can be asked to imagine a piece six pages in length that was notated like the first example above. All of those required triplet and sextuplet indications would certainly clutter up the pages, especially when dynamic markings, accents, slurs, ties, accidentals, bowing indications, and the like were added. Someone had to find a different and "cleaner" way to put the music on paper when the one-count sounds were predominately divided into three and six equal parts instead of two and four. All of those bothersome little numbers and grouping brackets had to be eliminated. But how was that to be done?

Those who designed our system of musical notation could have simply added more note symbols, and the problem would have been solved centuries ago. For example, triplet indications like those above would not be necessary if there were simply *third* notes in music. Why not? If we have *half* notes and *quarter* notes, why can't we have *third* notes and *sixth* notes?

We are probably all thankful that the solution did not involve adding more note symbols. I personally find "the big five" -- whole, half, quarter, eighth, and sixteenth notes -- to be more than enough for students to deal with. I also can't help but wonder what one-third, two-thirds, sixth, and even twelfth notes might look like. Whatever their look, I feel very certain that they would make music reading much more difficult. In my opinion, creating more note symbols would be a case of the solution becoming a bigger problem than the problem. Give me those little numbers any day, thank you. But, of course, none of that was necessary because of *the power of the dot.*

The Power of the Dot

As our students are introduced to musical notation in simple meters, they experience dotted notes. Dotted half notes and dotted quarter notes in 2/4, 3/4, and 4/4 are very familiar to them. They have most likely been informed that the dot adds half of the value of the note to the note but, in truth, many do not really understand what that means. "Adding half of the value of the note to the note" is verbally confusing. Because the dot is the key to understanding compound meter notation, students must gain a thorough knowledge of the dot and what it does. One thing they *must* understand is that *inside every dotted note live three notes.* They need to learn this early in their studies and hear it repeated often throughout them. For young students, a picture may, indeed, be worth a thousand words.

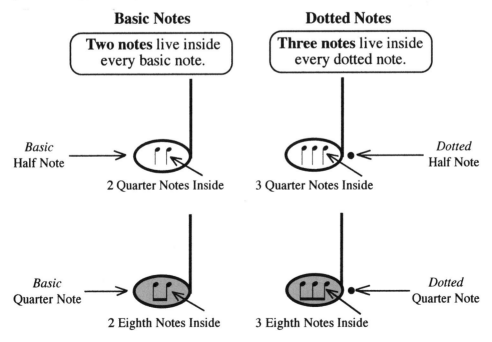

As they grow in their understanding of music notation, our students need to know the *natural division of all note symbols*. The natural division of all *basic* notes is into *two* equal parts. The natural division of all *dotted* notes is into *three* equal parts.

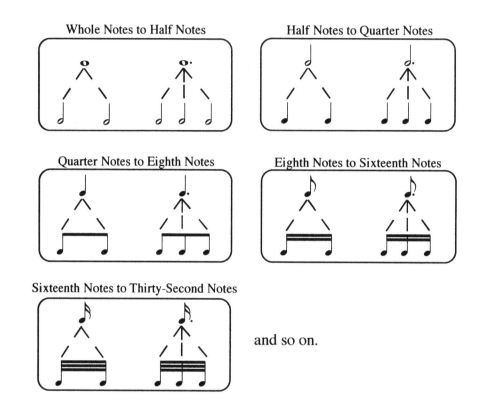

and so on.

The Family of Notes

As was discussed briefly on pages 110 and 111, all of the note symbols in music are derived from and dependent upon the whole note. The whole note is the head of a **Family of Notes**. This family has both visual and mathematical relationships. Not all notes have stems or are filled in or have flags and beams but, visually, they all retain the original oval shape of the whole note, from which they all descended. All note names are derived from their mathematical relationship to the whole note. A half note is 1/2 the value of the whole note. A quarter note is 1/4 the value of the whole note, and so on. Therefore, all note values in a piece of music are derived from the value of the whole note. Starting with the whole note, each new note symbol in this family of notes has a value that is one-half the value of the note before it.

Family of Basic Notes
When the *Whole Note* Equals Four Counts

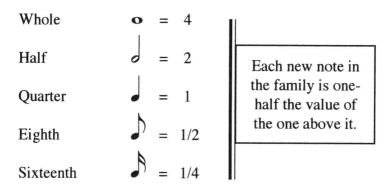

Whole	𝅝	=	4	
Half	𝅗𝅥	=	2	Each new note in the family is one-half the value of the one above it.
Quarter	𝅘𝅥	=	1	
Eighth	𝅘𝅥𝅮	=	1/2	
Sixteenth	𝅘𝅥𝅯	=	1/4	

Many of us have perhaps never given it a thought, but a closely related family of notes, **The Family of *Dotted* Notes**, consists of the exact same relationships.

Family of Dotted Notes
When the *Dotted* Whole Note Equals Four Counts

Dotted Whole	𝅝.	=	4	
Dotted Half	𝅗𝅥.	=	2	Each new note in the family is one-half the value of the one above it.
Dotted Quarter	𝅘𝅥.	=	1	
Dotted Eighth	𝅘𝅥𝅮.	=	1/2	
Dotted Sixteenth	𝅘𝅥𝅯.	=	1/4	

The Solution to the Problem of Notating Compound Rhythms

Although the mathematics of the "Family of *Dotted* Notes" pictured above is accurate and true, it only partially helped to solve the problem of compound notation. We will see shortly that the top three notes in the above graphic -- the dotted whole, dotted half, and dotted quarter -- were very helpful and useful. But dotted eighth notes that are one-half-of-a-count and dotted sixteenth notes that are one-fourth-of-a-count are not only confusing, but they serve no practical purpose. Writing notes with those values is very easily done using the basic notation system based on *division by twos*. Finding another way to write notes with those values was not necessary. On the other hand, finding a way to notate 1/3 and 2/3 and 1/6 count notes was essential and, as it turns out, the solution was just sitting there, waiting to be discovered.

Based on the knowledge that, within any given dotted note there exists the equivalent of three notes, a very creative thinker several centuries ago solved the problem of compound notation. He or she reasoned that, when composers wanted to inform performers that the predominate division of the one-beat sounds in a composition was into three equal parts instead of two, they simply needed to designate that *a dotted note was the note to get one beat*. If the one-beat note was a dotted note, the three notes that live inside that dotted note could be written without the *"3"* being required. A dotted note *naturally* divides into three equal parts. It is not an exception; it is the rule. Thus, compound notation was born -- a simple and elegant solution to a bothersome problem. Make the one-beat note a dotted note, and the problem is solved.

A Comparison of Simple and Compound Notation
Four Beats in the Measure

Simple Meter	Compound Meter
4/4	**12/8**
o = 4	o· = 4
𝅗𝅥 = 2	𝅗𝅥· = 2
♩ = 1	(♩· = 1)
♫ = 1 (1/2+1/2)	♫♪ = 1 (1/3+1/3+1/3)
♬♬ = 1 (1/4+1/4+1/4+1/4)	= 1 (1/6+1/6+1/6+1/6+1/6+1/6)

A chalkboard, bulletin board, or worksheet visual like the one on the previous page allows students to *see* why the triplet sounds in 12/8 do not require the special triplet marking that the same sounds in 4/4 would require. Triplet eighth notes in 4/4 can certainly be written and performed, but they are an exception and must be labeled as such. In compound 12/8, triplet eighth notes are a naturally occurring phenomenon, because the one-beat sound is a dotted quarter note. By simply decreeing that the one-beat note had to be a dotted note in compound meter, the problems associated with notating it were solved. Ingenious!

Defining the Word "Compound"

The following is not a conversation that would likely take place in an elementary school classroom. However, advanced middle school and high school and certainly music theory classes would benefit from it. To fully understand compound meter, students need to know the meaning of the word "compound" as it is used in music.

There are many definitions of compound meter. Most of them can be condensed into something like, "The beats in compound meter are divided into three instead of two equal parts." This is obviously true but, in my view, it is basically *describing* compound meter rather than *defining* it. I have for a long time puzzled about why someone several centuries ago would choose the word "compound" as the label for this music. As they experienced music similar to our "Over the River and Through the Woods" or "Seventy-Six Trombones," and the like, what is it about it that might lead them to exclaim, "I know what we can call this music -- compound!" Why that particular word? What does it mean? What is compound about this music? I believe that any definition of compound meter needs to address the word "compound" itself.

Many seem to believe that it is called compound because of the underlying, added note inherent in the notation. The graphic on the previous page clearly shows that the one-beat sounds of compound meter contain the equivalent of an added note. The one-beat note in 4/4 contains two eighth notes, while the one-beat note in 12/8 has the value of three eighth notes. It would seem that the two eighth notes have been *compounded* to a total of three eighth notes. Others state that 6/8 is compound, because it is the adding together of two measures of 3/8 (3/8+3/8=6/8). I would have to guess that, using that definition, 3/8 by itself is not compound meter. Yet the beats in 3/8 ($\quarternote. = 120$) are clearly divided into threes. I do not believe that these definitions go to the fundamental meaning of the term "*compound* meter."

Let's stop thinking about music for awhile and focus just on the English language. What is a compound? In chemistry, it is the combining of two separate and different elements to create something new. One molecule of water (H_2O) is the result of combining two atoms of hydrogen with one atom of oxygen. Water does not result from simply adding a third atom of hydrogen to the existing two. That would only result in three atoms of hydrogen. It would not be a compound, and it would not create something new. In language, a compound word is the result of combining two different words to create a new word. "Butterfly" is a good example. Butter and fly are two perfectly understood words. Combining them together into one word does not result in something you spread on toast that lands on your breakfast table by the rapid fluctuation of its wings, however. The two different words were compounded into a single word with a new meaning. In banking, compound interest is the adding together of two different financial elements, principal and interest, to create a new sum that becomes the new principal amount to be used to calculate the next cycle of compound interest.

It seems clear that the important and recurring word in the above definitions is the word *different*. A binary compound, that is, the combining of two separate elements into a single compound, results in something new and different than the two individual and separate elements. To define compound meter in music, then, we need to answer this question: What two, different elements were combined to create this new and different notation?

The answer involves compound meter's mathematical structure. Compound meter notation resulted from the combining of music with a mathematical ratio of 2:1 and music with a mathematical ratio of 3:1 into a single system. This combining of two different ratios resulted in a new notation. Simple meter music, as we have seen, maintains a mathematical ratio of 2:1 throughout its entire structure. Every new note in the "Family of *Basic* Notes" has a 2:1 relationship with the note from which it descended. Once again we will use 4/4 and 12/8 for purposes of comparison.

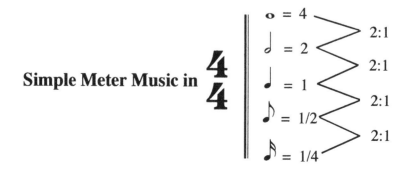

Compound meter notation combines selected elements from the two different note families mentioned previously -- the "Family of *Basic* Notes" and the "Family of *Dotted* Notes." In the case of 12/8 below, the top three system components are from the "Family of *Dotted* Notes" -- the dotted whole, the dotted half, and the dotted quarter. All of the remaining, beginning with the eighth note, are from the "Family of *Basic* Notes." Mathematically, the notes in this combined system also have a 2:1 ratio with each other *except for one important instance*. At the place where the two families meet, a 3:1 ratio occurs. The one-beat note in this new system does not divide into two parts. It divides into three parts.

Compound Meter Music in 12/8

$$o\cdot = 4$$
$$\text{♩}\cdot = 2 \quad \text{2:1}$$
$$\text{♩}\cdot = 1 \quad \text{2:1}$$
$$\text{♪} = 1/3 \quad \text{(3:1)}$$
$$\text{♪} = 1/6 \quad \text{2:1}$$

Why was this new notation named "compound?" Because it meets all of the criteria for a compound. It not only combines known elements from the two different families of notes but, most importantly, it combines two different mathematical ratios into one system. In chemistry, atoms of hydrogen and oxygen combine to create water. In music, mathematical ratios of 2:1 and 3:1 combine to create compound meter notation. This new notation was, indeed, a compound and was, therefore, appropriately named.

Composer's Dilemma: Simple or Compound Notation?

Our students may be curious to know why a composer chooses simple over compound notation or vise versa when writing a piece of music. Since the same sounds can technically be notated either way, what dictates the chosen mode for a composer? The answer is fairly simple. Most pieces of music have a *predominate* feeling of either beats divided into twos or beats divided into threes. If the overall feeling of the music is a feeling of beats divided by threes, then the composer is likely to choose to write in compound meter, most commonly 3/8 or 6/8 or 9/8 or 12/8. If a few of the one-beat sounds in the piece are divided into only two parts, those exceptions will be notated as duplets with the appropriate *"2"* indicated under or over them. And, of course, the opposite is true.

The same thing can be said in a simpler way for younger students. A composer will choose the meter that results in the fewest number of exceptions that require the little numbers under or over note groupings.

Is This 6/8 Piece in Six or in Two?

Because it is probably the most frequently seen of the compound meters, we are using 6/8 as our example. Obviously, the following questions are equally legitimate: Is this 3/8 piece in three or in one? Is this 9/8 piece in nine or in three? Is this 12/8 piece in twelve or in four? Simply stated, students need to know whether the value of each eighth note is one count or one-third- of-a-count. It is very important that students eventually be able to answer these kinds of questions without our help. Their ability to do so will determine how well they will be able to interpret the meanings of the numbers in time signatures, a subject to be discussed shortly.

Students who understand that the one-beat note in all compound meters *must be a dotted note* should look first for a metronome marking. This is absolutely the most certain way for a performer to know that the composer intended for the music to be "fast 6/8 -- *in 2*." If the metronome marking is ♩.= 120 , the piece is, without question, in compound meter. On the other hand, if the metronome marking is ♪= 120 , the piece is in six beats to the measure, what some would call "slow 6/8." Even though we might consider 120 beats per minute to be a somewhat fast tempo, the metronome marking has made it clear that the eighth note is the note to receive one count. The music is definitely in six, and its meter is simple, not compound.

If there is no metronome marking, some compositions in 6/8 will actually have printed on the manuscript *"in 2"* or *"in 6."* Students can also be taught to look for musical terms that refer to tempo. If a 6/8 piece is marked *allegro* or *march tempo,* the composer intended it to be played fast, in two. On the other hand, if the tempo marking is *largo,* the piece will sound as the composer intended if it is performed with six beats in each measure. If a piece is marked *moderato* or *andante,* the student may need to look further for the answer.

If none of the above helps to answer the question, students should be encouraged to play or sing it both ways, in six and in two, and then decide for themselves which sounded more appropriate and musical to their ears. Students who begin to make these kinds of musical value judgements on their own are becoming musically mature.

Duple and Triple Meter

You have perhaps noticed that throughout this book, the common musical terms "duple" and "triple" have been avoided. Some musicians would label our "beats divided into twos" as music in *duple* meter. "Beats divided into threes" would be described as music in *triple* meter. I have decided not to use those terms, however, because they seem very often to morph into more complex descriptions having to do with overall metrical patterns, the number of beats per measure, and so forth. I believe that too much of the duple and triple verbiage that we use in music lends itself to needless confusion in young minds. In my view, it is much easier and, therefore, much more successful if students first learn that a composition's meter is one of two things -- either simple or compound, depending on how the one-beat notes are divided. Students who undertake an in-depth study of music theory later on will likely benefit from studying terms such as *simple triple, compound duple, simple sextuple,* and the like. The majority of our students do not need that information, but they do need to know if the music is in simple or compound meter if they are to successfully navigate the music they will encounter in our music programs.

3/4 Time: Simple or Compound?

Too many of our students incorrectly come to assume that all music in 3/8, 6/8, 9/8, and 12/8 is in compound meter. It is true that much of the music that students encounter in those meters will be compound, but not all. A far greater number of our students assume that any time signature with a "4" on the bottom indicates simple meter. Not so. Students need to be reminded that meter cannot be determined by looking only at the time signature. Each individual piece needs to be analyzed for meter.

3/4 is an interesting example of this phenomenon. Most students would assume that music written in 3/4 is in simple meter, and most of the time they would be correct.

The one-beat notes above are divided into two equal halves. The triplet eighth notes are an exception to that and are marked accordingly. The metronome marking enables us to know precisely what the composer intended. Quarter notes are one count. This is unquestionably simple meter music.

Even though the notes and rhythms below are identical to the ones we just looked at, this version is definitely in compound meter. The indication *"in 1"* tells us that the dotted half note is the one-beat note. The three quarter notes in the first measure are the natural three-part division of the one-beat note. The triplet eighth notes are still an exception and must be marked, because the natural division of the quarter note is into two parts, not three.

The above is a good example of 3/4 *waltz time*. We need to make certain that our students understand that compound meter does not require an "8" as the bottom number of the time signature, even though that is what they will see most often. Students who fully understand compound meter notation should be able to perform any 3/4 piece *"in 1,"* if their director requests it.

A Compound Meter Counting System

As in simple meters, there are also many counting systems in existence for music in compound meters. *Trip-o-let, 1-la-li, Du-da-di, Tri-o-la, 1-trip-let,* among others. Those of you who have read this book from the beginning know that a "number-counting" system is going to be recommended here. The rationale for that is detailed on pages 124-140. Counting systems that use numbers are more apt to challenge students to analyze individual rhythmic figures and how they function in a specific setting. Numbers help teachers to know that students are analyzing rhythms correctly. The use of numbers helps students to coordinate what they see on the paper with the beat points of the conductor's baton.

Two of the more popular number-counting systems for compound meters are based on *1-la-li* and *1-trip-let*. When discussing triplets in simple meters, the reason we prefer the *1-trip-let* system was earlier stated this way:

"Triplets in simple meters are recited as *1-trip-let 2 trip-let,* and so forth. These lyrics are preferred to the perhaps more common *1-la-li 2-la-li* for the following simple reason. When students are trying to work out a rhythm on their own and they see the number *"3"* written above or below the triplet figure, they are more likely to recall the counting word *trip-let* than they are the neutral syllables *la-li*. "Triplet" seems to be the more logical choice. Students *see* triplet and they *say* "trip-let." Of course, the number identifies the count on which the triplet resides."

Defining the Word "Triplet"

Many students' first exposure to three notes evenly spaced over one beat is by way of simple meters -- 2/4 or 4/4 being the most likely time signatures. Too often students form an incorrect understanding of triplets. Because they first experience them in 4/4, for example, they think that triplets must have the grouping number *"3"* above or below the three notes in order to be triplets. This is an incorrect assumption. Once again we need to first focus student attention on the *sound* of the music, and then the notation. If I were listening to a piece of music with an overwhelming number of triplet sounds, I might ask myself, "Do I hear triplets?" I would not respond with, "I don't know. I'll have to see the music before I can know that." If they sound like triplets, they are triplets. They could be notated several different ways, but the form of the notation will not change the fact that they are triplets. Students need to know that eighth notes grouped in threes in compound 6/8 are triplets. They will be counted as triplets, but there will be no little number *"3"* on the paper as an identifier. Notation does not cause triplets; it represents them. It's all in the sound.

Counting Systems Model Performance

As was stated previously, we use counting systems to model rhythmic performance, not to demonstrate student understanding. Therefore, two rhythms that sound the same must use the exact same rhythm lyrics, no matter how they look on paper. Our counting systems need to be all about the sounds of the rhythms.

And so it stands to reason that, whether students are counting triplet rhythms in simple or in compound notation, the same rhythmic sounds must be spoken using the same lyrics. If they say *1-trip-let* in simple meters, students must say *1-trip-let* in compound meters, even though they look different.

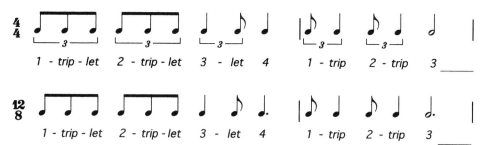

Numbers NOT To Be Used
in Compound Meter

I am very certain that teaching students to count compound meter using simple meter lyrics is very confusing for students. In this case, the use of numbers will tend to do more harm than good. Consider the following:

The metronome marking clearly tells us that this music is in compound meter, but the students are counting in simple meter, giving each eighth note one count. If asked by the teacher, the students would be able to identify that the note "F" is on count four, but there is no four on the director's conducting pattern. Actually there is no four anywhere in the piece. There are clearly only two beats per measure in this music. If we encourage students to count from the numbers one through six in measures that have only two beats, we are really not making much sense in students' minds. When we try to explain to students that there are six *counts* but only two *beats* per measure, we lose many of them. Yes, we take the time necessary to explain it to our own satisfaction but, to students, it is just another episode of meaningless teacher talk. Because we are already accomplished musicians, it is not easy for us to hear just how convoluted it really sounds to students. We understand what we mean, but many of our students don't, and they are the important ones.

The problem with using simple meter lyrics with compound notation becomes even more troublesome when counting sixteenth notes in 6/8. I once observed an excellent high school band that was having difficulty with a piece in compound 6/8. The upper woodwinds had measure after measure of sixteenth note scale figures, and they just weren't getting it. The fingerings and the speed were not the problem. They just couldn't seem to hear how it fit rhythmically. The teacher asked the students to count the passage aloud, up to tempo, so that they could hear what it should sound like.

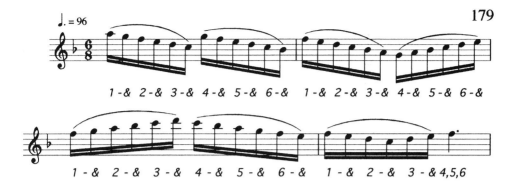

At the given tempo of ♩. = 96 , try counting the above example aloud. It is next to impossible to say those words that fast and accurately. I can't begin to get anywhere near tempo. The situation in the classroom actually became rather amusing. It was like the entire class had entered a "Tongue Twisting" contest but hadn't practiced nearly enough. Because this was not the kind of class in which you felt free to laugh when the teacher was serious, many students suddenly seemed to develop coughing fits -- any excuse to put their hands over their faces, so that the teacher couldn't see that they thought the whole thing was hilarious. It was really quite funny, but also sad at the same time. The students were not getting the help they needed. The teacher had asked them to count it so they could hear how it should sound, but the counting words made that impossible.

In my own teaching, I discovered some counting words for situations like the above that not only solved the problem, but that also helped students develop a firmer grasp on the workings of compound meter. Consider the following.

Counting Sixteenths in Compound 6/8

Once again, 6/8 is the example I will be using. It goes without saying that everything applies equally well to compound 3/8, 9/8, 12/8. 15/8, and so on.

Students must first understand that each pair of sixteenth notes in these time signatures evolves from the natural splitting of individual triplet eighth notes. When this occurs, the "extra" note is pronounced *"a,"* the exact same sound as the *"a"* in *1-e-&-a* (pronounced like the first syllable of the word *other*).

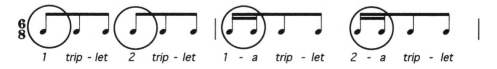

Students who see a rhythm like that one simply need to analyze that the first eighth note of both triplets has been split into two sixteenths. Visually, this is quite easy to see because of the way the notes are beamed. Therefore, instead of pronouncing the first eighth note's place in the second measure as a simple *"1,"* it becomes *"1-a,"* said twice as fast, of course. In the following examples, the eighth notes *"trip"* become the sixteenth notes *"trip-a,"* and the eighth notes *"let"* become the sixteenth notes *"let-a."* Chant the following aloud.

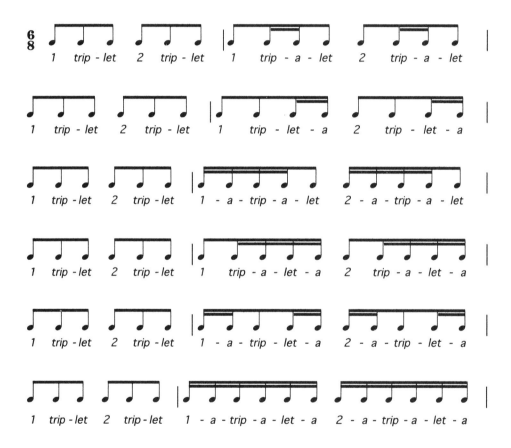

On the example below, it is the second eighth note that is split. The dot of the dotted eighth is the unpronounced *"trip,"* and the sixteenth is the *"a"* of *"trip-a."*

This particular counting system constantly reinforces in students' minds the fact that the fundamental rhythm of compound 6/8 is the triplet. Two sixteenth notes can naturally evolve from any or all of the eighth notes in the triplet figure, and those sixteenths retain the counting name of the specific eighth note from which they came. Additionally, the words seem to flow off the tongue effortlessly and lightly. The scale passage from before can easily be spoken up to tempo, giving the students the help they need to "hear" the passage. With very little practice, it can be said even faster. Try it.

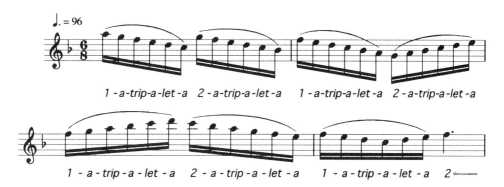

Because all of the counting lyrics suggested here for compound meter are derived from the same basic foundation, -- that is, *numbers* and the word *triplet,* they can be used to terrific advantage in situations like the upper woodwind scale passages above. You recall that the students could finger the scales and could play them up to tempo, but they were having difficulty hearing how they fit together rhythmically. The band director could divide the entire ensemble into four rhythm groups and orchestrate the following drum-like chant to wonderful effect. The entire band becomes a percussion ensemble. It would work best if the lyrics were spoken crisply, more of a light staccato type of articulation.

Director: *(After dividing the band into four groups)*

Group One: You are our "keepers of the beat." Your part is simple but very important. Try this with me.

♩. = 96

$^{6}_{8}$ 𝅘𝅥𝅮 𝄾 𝄾 𝅘𝅥𝅮 𝄾 𝄾 | 𝅘𝅥𝅮 𝄾 𝄾 𝅘𝅥𝅮 𝄾 𝄾 |
     1   2   1   2

They practice a couple measures and then are stopped, as the next group receives its assignment.

Group Two: When I cue you in, chant this rhythm. Speak your words very precisely and crisply. Try it.

The two groups are briefly rehearsed together, with attention drawn to the fact that the numbers "1" and "2" are spoken at the exact same instant.

Group Three: Here is your part. Join me.

$$\frac{6}{8} \quad \text{♪♪♪ ♪♪♪ | ♪♪♪ ♪♪♪ |}$$
1 trip-let 2 trip-let 1 trip-let 2 trip-let

The three groups are briefly rehearsed, listening for the simultaneous speaking of the numbers and the syllable "let."

Group Four (the upper woodwinds): When I cue you, join us with your sixteenth note counting from rehearsal number 78.

Before we put this together, band, we all need to be aware of the fact that, if we are very accurate rhythmically, all of our common words will line up perfectly. These words will be heard at the exact, same split second: *"1" - "trip" - "let" - "2" - "trip" - and "let."* And the *"a's"* spoken by the upper woodwinds will always be heard by themselves. Listen for that.

Watch me for dynamics. We'll start *piano* and gradually *crescendo*, and then end like we started -- *piano*.

Let's try it now. I'll cue each group when to start and when to stop. Group One, you start us out -- *piano*.

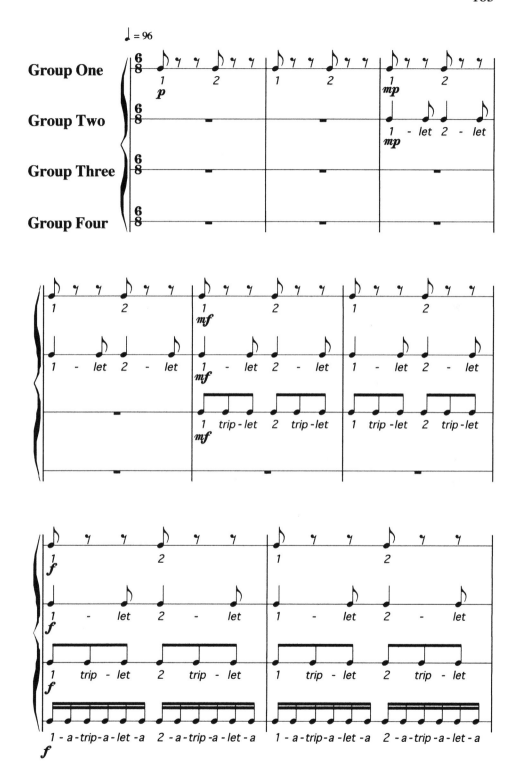

p

The exercise could then be repeated immediately with one change. The upper woodwinds could *play* their part at rehearsal number 78, as the rest of the band continued to act as their percussion section.

These same kinds of rehearsal techniques can be used with other counting systems and in simple meter as well, provided that the spoken components of the chosen counting system are all derived from the same sources, so that the same words line up vertically as these do. In this particular case the counting words *"1-trip-let"* probably work better than *"1-la-li,"* simply because of the more percussive articulation of the syllables *"trip-let"* compared to the more legato sounds of *"la-li."* Turning entire bands, orchestras, and choirs into percussion ensembles is both educational and enjoyable. Rhythmic chanting, when done well, is a musical experience with benefits.

The Meanings of the Numbers in Compound Time Signatures

A discussion with students concerning the meanings of the numbers in compound time signatures is best left until the students are competent in the reading and performance of compound music. Ideally time signature questions will not arise until such time as the explanation is likely to be understood by all students, because the explanation *reflects* and *confirms* the experience. Attempting to teach these concepts before students have been properly prepared to accept them will not be productive. Students will best understand the theory after they have mastered the performance.

This book has clearly advocated a different approach to the initial introduction of the meanings of the top and bottom numbers in time signatures. The key to this new approach is a new and different understanding of the bottom numbers in simple time signatures. Our younger students are far more likely to comprehend the meanings of the numbers when they are introduced to them in the following manner:

When the time signature is $\frac{4}{4}$,

The total number of counts in each full measure will be **4**
based on a ***whole note value*** of **4**

The whole note is the most important note for students to know and is the note that determines all note values in a piece of music in simple meter. For a complete review of these concepts, see pages 75-113.

Although we strongly suggest that students be *introduced* to time signature theory in this new way, we do state that students need to *later* become acquainted with the traditional explanation of the meaning of the bottom numbers in time signatures. The bottom number of the time signature represents *a kind of note*. On pages 114 and 115, it was stated this way:

> "Make no mistake about it. Students do eventually need to be taught the traditional meaning of the bottom numbers in time signatures in order to function in the musical world. *This does not create a problem.* Students who have received a thorough grounding in the system that is advocated here have no difficulty assimilating both definitions into one cohesive package when they are older and are able to view things from more than one perspective...... When they are more mature, students can look at the bottom number of a simple time signature and realize that it represents both the value of the whole note, and it signifies the kind of note that gets one count at the same time. In fact, the two definitions actually validate each other. When the bottom number is four, they know that whole notes are four counts, half notes are two and, of course, quarter notes are one count. There is no conflict. Students are free to think about it from whichever perspective they prefer. However, when it comes time for students to understand the meanings of the numbers in *compound* time signatures, they will need to know that the bottom number of the time signature stands for a kind of a note."

Our system of rhythmic notation was designed to symbolize music in which the beats are *divided by twos*. To make it work for beats *divided by threes* requires that certain compromises be made, not only in notation, but in the meanings of the numbers in time signatures as well.

"The top number of the time signature tells us how many counts are in a measure, and the bottom number tells us what kind of a note gets one count." This universally-known definition works very well for all *simple* meter music. Simple 6/8 is an example. One-count eighth notes naturally divide into half-count sixteenths, which are counted *1-& 2-&, 3-&,* and so forth. There truly are six counts in a measure, and the eighth notes do get one count, just like the traditional definition indicates. But that same definition absolutely does not work for compound 6/8 music. There are not six counts in a measure in this music. There are only two, because eighth notes do not get one count. They get one-third of a count. If we introduce our students to a 6/8 march, reminding them that there are six counts in a measure and the eighth note gets one count, they are hearing what many of them consider to be rhythmic gibberish. They don't understand it and what's worse, in many cases, they don't want to. Unfortunately, because we understand the material so well, it is difficult for us to truly appreciate how genuinely confusing it sounds to our students. Many of them who hear something that sounds confusing are too quick to say, "I don't get it." They close their minds to even trying. Clearly, if the majority of our students are to understand it, we should not attempt to have one definition fit both meters. Applying a simple meter definition of the numbers in time signatures to music written in compound meter defies logic. It needlessly confuses students. It is understood only by those who already have a thorough background in rhythm theory. That is obviously not the audience we are addressing as we attempt to teach this material.

Students cannot know which definition of the numbers in time signatures to apply to a piece of music until they determine whether the music is in simple or compound meter. When students look at a piece of music and determine that the basic counting in the piece is *1-&, 2-&*, and so forth, the piece is in simple meter, regardless of the time signature. The meaning of the numbers in time signatures for this kind of music is either:

a) The top number indicates the number of counts per measure.
   The bottom number indicates the value of the whole note, or
b) The top number indicates the number of counts per measure.
   The bottom number stands for the kind of note that gets one count.

When students look at a piece of music and determine that the basic counting in the piece is *1-trip-let, 2-trip-let*, and so forth, the piece is in compound meter, regardless of the time signature. This music calls for a different meaning of the numbers in the time signature.

Basically, the numbers in compound time signatures indicate *how many* (the top number) of *what kind of note* (the bottom number) fit into a full measure of music. For example:

In compound 3/8,
    there are the equivalent of **3**
                                          8th notes per measure.

Once it has been determined that the music is in compound rather than simple meter, the students know that the three eighth notes that fit in one measure would not be counted *1,2,3*. One full measure of eighth notes ($\frac{3}{8}$ ♩♩♩ |) would be counted *1-trip-let*. Therefore, in compound 3/8, there is one count per measure. This time signature is often referred to as *3/8 in 1*.

In compound 6/8,
there are the equivalent of **6**
8th notes per measure.

Because the students have already confirmed that the music is in compound meter, they know that the six eighth notes would be grouped into two sets of three and would be counted *1-trip-let, 2-trip-let*. Therefore, in compound 6/8, there are two counts per measure. This time signature is often referred to as *6/8 in 2*.

In compound 9/8,
there are the equivalent of **9**
8th notes per measure.

Because the students have already confirmed that the music is in compound meter, they know that the nine eighth notes would be grouped into three sets of three and would be counted *1-trip-let, 2-trip-let, 3-trip-let*. Therefore, in compound 9/8, there are three counts per measure. This time signature is often referred to as *9/8 in 3*.

In compound 12/8,
there are the equivalent of **12**
8th notes per measure.

Because the students have already confirmed that the music is in compound meter, they know that the twelve eighth notes would be grouped into four sets of three and would be counted *1-trip-let, 2-trip-let, 3-trip-let, 4-trip-let*. Therefore, in compound 12/8, there are four counts per measure. This time signature is often referred to as *12/8 in 4*.

In compound 3/4,
there are the equivalent of **3**
4th (quarter) notes per measure.

Because the students have already confirmed that the music is in compound meter, they know that the three quarter notes would be a threesome and a full measure of them would be counted *1-trip-let*. In compound 3/4, there is one count per measure. This time signature is often referred to as *3/4 in 1* or *waltz time*.

Additionally, students can be taught that, in compound meter, the top number of the time signature *must* be a number evenly divisible by three -- 3, 6, 9, 12, 15, and so forth. They should be cautioned, however, that this does not guarantee that the music is compound. Any compound-looking time signature can also represent music in simple meter. Once again, it comes down to a question of how the one-beat note is divided. If the one-beat divided notes are counted *1-&*, the music is in simple meter. If the one-beat divided notes are counted *1-trip-let,* the music is in compound meter.

Once students are made aware of the fact that the top number of a piece in compound meter must be a multiple of three, they can be shown how to quickly figure out how many beats will be in each measure and, therefore, which conducting pattern they will see from their director. They simply need to divide the top number of the time signature by three. If the top number is three, the piece is *"in 1"* (3 ÷ 3 = 1). If the top number is six, there are two beats a measure, and so forth.

Rhythmic Literacy in Compound Meter

In order for students to be assessed as literate in compound meter, they need to be able to *read* the language, *perform* it musically at sight, *write* it correctly, and demonstrate skill at taking *dictation* in it. If this seems like an imposing list, remember that these skills are not introduced and implemented all at once. They are introduced early and reinforced consistently over an extended period of time. Does this take away rehearsal time? Yes, but not an excessive amount if literacy sessions are thoughtfully and well-planned. Does it result in a better musical experience for students? Absolutely. In language arts classes, persons who have to stop and sound out every third word in a poem cannot reasonably be expected to be touched by the poet's message. It is lost in the tiresome and frustrating working-out of the words. In music classes, students who have achieved rhythmic literacy are able to spend more of their time being touched by the *music* rather than by working-out the *rhythms*. It was stated before and bears repeating: There are some things for which time must simply be taken.

Students' earliest experiences writing in compound meter should involve writing notes that are not divided -- in other words, one, two, three, and four-count notes. A few, short examples follow, the first of which could easily be done by very young students when they are first being introduced to compound meter. Each of these examples could be expanded into an entire worksheet. Worksheets that have students writing compound notation could be assigned as homework, so as to not take away from rehearsal time, although it is not possible to know for certain that the students did the work themselves. Even so, written homework assignments in our classes are highly recommended. They help both students and parents to understand that what we teach is a serious undertaking that is both *aesthetic and academic*. It is not entertainment. Students and parents need to know that grading in our classes will partially depend on the individual student's degree of understanding of the material being presented in the course, just as in math, science, language arts, and social studies. For this reason, sometime during every grading period, we need to administer in-class written quizzes or exams. If we are to achieve the much-desired status of an academic subject in the eyes of the community, we need to occasionally employ some standard academic tools -- written homework and the written test.

The importance of the first samples of literacy lessons that follow is that students have to dot the one, two, three, and four-count notes in compound meters. One of the most frequently made mistakes by students writing in these meters is leaving off the dot, and the dotted note is the key to understanding compound meter. We can continually remind students of this, or we can have them write the dots after the notes themselves. In my mind, there is no doubt about which is the more significant method of presenting this material. Students remember what they do far better than they remember what they are told. Our students need to write in compound meters.

******

Fill in each blank measure below with the exact same sounds as the measure before it. Each pair of measures should sound the same.

More advanced example: Fill in each blank measure below with the same sounds as the measure before it. Your measures must be written in *compound meter*. Be sure to write in the correct compound time signature for each of your measures. Each pair of measures should sound exactly the same.

Rewrite the following familiar song, so that both versions sound alike. If you know the title of the song, fill it in. Write your music neatly, so that someone could play or sing your version of the song without difficulty.

Title: _____

******

After students have been introduced to the notation associated with divided beats in compound meter, more advanced worksheets, quizzes, and exams are recommended. One possible example follows:

******

Rewrite the etude below, so that your version sounds exactly like the printed version. Check your work.

192

This final example would likely be more appropriate for late middle school or high school students.

*****

Instructions

Rewrite the etude below, so that your version would sound exactly the same as the given one.

******

Correct Responses

Episodes of rhythmic dictation can follow the same path as the ideas for written work outlined above. They can start very simply with undivided beats in compound meter. Then gradually the sounds of triplets can be used. A rhythmic dictation shorthand like that described on page 43 can be implemented if desired. After students demonstrate competency in compound meter dictation, they can be expected to take rhythmic dictation in mixed meters.

******

Teacher: This will be only two measures, but in mixed meters. The first measure is in a compound meter, the second in simple. Be sure to write in the time signatures. I will repeat it four times. *The teacher chants the rhythm on neutral syllables while clapping or tapping the beat loudly enough for students to clearly discern it.* Advanced students could be instructed to show the "beat equivalency" between the two measures.

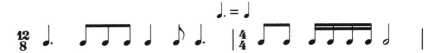

Note: Although highly unlikely, a student could notate the dictation as follows, since the instructions did not require specific time signatures.

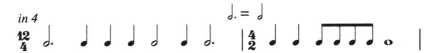

We all need to remember that the same sounds can be notated differently.

Part Five

Introducing Students
to
Irregular Meter

Although the one-beat notes are divided differently in simple and compound meters, the beats themselves are steady unless changed by expressive markings such as ritardando, accelerando, rubato, and the like. This concept of steady beat is critical to the development of musicianship. One of the earliest and most vital music skills for very young children to acquire is the establishment of a feeling of steady beat. Many believe that if steady beat is not internalized at a young age, it may never come.

There is a third classification of meter that students need to learn as they advance in their musicianship. The introduction to this type of meter should not occur until the steady-beat meters, simple and compound, are mastered. The most noticeable characteristic of this new class of meters is the fact that the beats are decidedly *unsteady*. They do not occur at regular and predictable intervals. The beats -- those things that the conductor conducts and the foot taps -- are **irregular**. Compare the three different settings of eighth notes that follow.

Simple Meter: Steady, *Regular* Beat

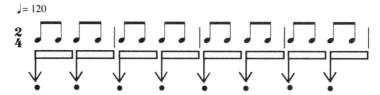

Compound Meter: Steady, *Regular* Beat

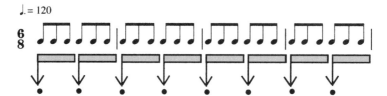

The beats in the above examples, represented by the rectangles, are precisely the same length. The two beats of each measure have a *symmetrical, balanced* look to them. They occur over regular, steady, and predictable intervals of time. Now compare those beats to the ones below.

Irregular Meter: Unsteady, *Irregular* Beat

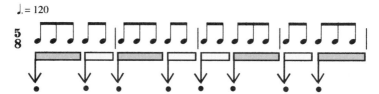

The two beats in each measure of this last example are not the same length. They have an *asymmetrical, unbalanced* look. The metronome marking dictates that the eighth notes cannot get the beat. The music is far too fast (♩.= 120) to be conducted or tapped in five. It must be conducted and performed in an *unbalanced* two, the longer and shorter beats being determined by each particular measure's notation. The resulting beats are irregular and unpredictable.

What we classify here as *irregular* meter is variously referred to as *asymmetric* meter, *complex* meter, *odd* meter, *combination* meter, and *composite* meter, among others. It does not matter which of these terms is employed to describe the meter, provided that the students understand the term, and that the same term is used consistently in the classroom. We choose to broadly classify these meters as **irregular**, because of that word's direct relationship to the meters' most identifiable characteristic. When students hear and feel irregular beats, they most easily recall and associate the term *irregular meter* with what they are experiencing. Irregular beat -- irregular meter. Younger students relate especially well to the idea that this music has an "irregular heart beat."

Combining Meters

Students are most likely to have their first encounter with irregular meter in literature that is written primarily in one of the steady beat meters, but that has occasional measures of irregular meter inserted to add rhythmic tension and interest. A short, representative example follows.

The irregular meter time signatures employed in this type of mixed meter composition are predominately measures of 3/8, 5/8, or 7/8, and probably less frequently 9/8 and 11/8. Because the top numbers of these representative time signatures are all odd numbers, many people logically choose to call these *odd* meters.

Once again we need to remind students that they cannot simply look at a time signature and, based upon the numbers, label the music as simple, compound, or irregular meter. All of the time signatures listed in the preceding paragraph will be simple meter when the eighth note gets the beat. 3/8 and 9/8 are very often compound meter. The music must always be examined in order to determine meter.

Fractional Time Signatures

******

Mr. Johnston is warming up his advanced middle school band. His intention during this warm-up session is to introduce the students to some of the combined meter compositional devices they will experience as they move on in the band program. He writes the following simple warm-up rhythm on the chalkboard and asks the students to play it up the Concert Bb Major Scale. The students repeat the measure until they reach the octave Bb.

Teacher: We're going to change this rhythm slightly. Watch what I do. I'll have some questions for you when I'm done. *He walks to the chalkboard and adds a fifth eighth note to the measure.*

Teacher: What do you think?

Michelle: You forgot to write in the *"3"* for the triplet.

Teacher: Good observation, Michelle, but I didn't want a triplet. I wanted exactly what you see. I intentionally wanted another half-count eighth note in the measure. Someone else?

Paul: Then you've made the measure wrong. It has two-and-a-half counts in it. That's too many.

Teacher: Exactly, Paul. What can we do about that, class?

Amber: Erase the extra eighth note!

Teacher: Well, yes. We could do that. It would make the measure correct again, wouldn't it? But that means we would have just been wasting our time, and we try hard not to do that in here. We need another solution to the problem. Anyone?

                He waits. No one offers a suggestion, so Mr. Johnston proposes something unusual.

Teacher: How about if we simply change the time signature? *He goes to the chalkboard and adds* $\frac{1}{2}$ *to the top number of the time signature.*

$2\frac{1}{2}$

The measure is now correct, right?

We're going to play this new rhythm, but before we do, you need to know that the added eighth note is *not* a downbeat. It is an extra *upbeat*. If it were a downbeat, it would be written as the first note in a beamed group. Before we changed the measure, it was counted *1 - & 2 - &*. With the added upbeat, we will need to add an extra "*&*" to the counting. Upbeats are always "&'s." I'll count the new measure several times. Join me when you are comfortable. Notice that all of the notes are recited evenly, at the exact same speed. That is because they are all the same kind of note -- half-count eighth notes. The last three notes may look like a triplet, but they are not. *He begins counting the measure. The students soon join in.*

When he sees that the students are counting the measure confidently, Mr. Johnson, without stopping and without explanation, begins clapping his hands on the counting numbers "1" and "2." He holds his left hand parallel to the floor, palm up. His right hand claps on a down-up axis. On the extended count 2, he allows his right hand to more or less just "float" up to account for the extra time required for count two. This is, of course, exactly how he will conduct count two with his baton. He indicates that the students should join him in clapping the beat, which they do.

Teacher: Terrific! Let's play this new rhythm up the scale. Be sure you tap your foot only on the downbeats, the numbers. Let your foot just *float up* on count two. Snare drummers, play all five, even eighth notes. Bass drummer, play only on the downbeats. Instruments up. Ready, play. *As the students play the scale, Mr. Johnston's conducting pattern emphasizes an upward-floating beat two, which mirrors their foot tapping.*

The next rehearsal begins with an exact replay of this one, but with an important difference. The students volunteer answers to the questions before they can be posed. When the teacher adds the extra eighth note, the students immediately inform him that he must change the top number of the time signature to $2\frac{1}{2}$. They demonstrate skill at both counting and playing the pattern. Their feet are tapping and the bass drum is sounding an irregular beat. The teacher is conducting an irregular, unbalanced pattern.

This is followed immediately by the teacher using eraser and chalk to change the beaming of the rhythm pattern on the board.

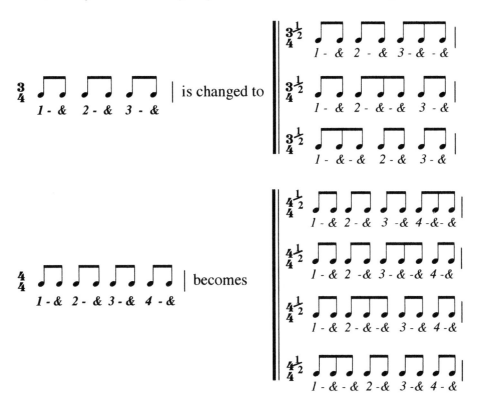

The students instantly recognize that count *one* now becomes the *long* beat. They successfully count and perform the pattern as *1 - & - & 2 - &*.

Over the next several rehearsals the students are guided, one step at a time, through the following sequence of short lessons in irregular meter.

Through experience, the students learn that any count can be the long one in these meters, and that it is the long one that causes the irregular beat.

With competence now established in the performance of irregular meter, it is time to prepare students for the way in which irregular meter, with its unsteady beat, will most likely be encountered in the literature. It is time to combine *steady-beat* music and *unsteady-beat* music into what many commonly call mixed meter.

******

Upon entering the room for rehearsal, the students notice that a very simple warm-up rhythm has been notated on the chalkboard. Near the beginning of the class, they are asked to play it up the scale, changing pitches at each barline.

The teacher makes certain that the last note in the exercise is played for only a half-count and that no note is added on the next downbeat. The students naturally want to end the exercise with a long note on the downbeat, but the teacher doesn't allow it. The students are learning to read what is written, not what they wish had been written.

The rhythm is immediately changed with the addition of one note and a new, added time signature in the fourth measure.

To make certain that the fourth measure is played accurately, Mr. Johnston gives the following instructions before the exercise is played.

Teacher: Snare drums, I want you to play steady eighth notes throughout the playing of this entire exercise. Bass drummer, of course, play on only the downbeats, as you always do. Band, to help you know the exact speed that the eighth notes will be when you get to them, listen carefully to the snare drum as you play the first two measures. Instruments up. Ready, play.

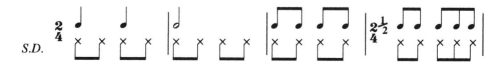

Teacher: Good job. When you were listening to the snare drums, you
                  were hearing what musicians refer to as *subdivision.* When-
                  ever musicians look ahead in their music and see shorter notes
                  coming up, they will often start to hear those shorter notes in
                  their heads before they get to that spot, so that they know
                  exactly what the shorter notes will sound like. *Subdividing*
                  now ensures accuracy later.

                  We're going to play this same exercise again, only this time
                  you will need to supply the snare drum part -- the *subdivi-*
                  sions -- yourself, because I am going to ask the snare drum-
                  mers not to play. While you are playing the first two mea-
                  sures, you will need to hear the steady *tick-tick-tick* of eighth
                  notes in your head. Ready play.

                                    ******

   Over the next several rehearsals, the students are given similar, short,
daily lessons involving mixed meter rhythm patterns played on the Bb scale.
For now, the time signatures of the measures of irregular meter are notated
as either: $1\frac{1}{2}\over 4$ or $2\frac{1}{2}\over 4$ or $3\frac{1}{2}\over 4$ or $4\frac{1}{2}\over 4$

This seems unusual, perhaps even strange to us, but to the students it is not.
They know of no other way of doing it, so to them, it seems normal, and it
makes sense. There are, in fact, one-and-a-half, two-and-a-half, three-and-a-
half, and four-and-a-half counts in the irregular meter measures.
   Students are consistently reminded of the value of subdividing the "long"
notes in order to play the eighth notes with complete accuracy. It is during
these lessons that the convention of ($\flat=\flat$) is introduced. Students are informed that if the eighth notes in the current measure are one-half count,
then the eighth notes in the new time signature are also one-half count. This
consistency in the value of the eighth note is the root cause of the irregular
beat.

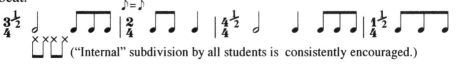

("Internal" subdivision by all students is consistently encouraged.)

   At this point, in order to help his students make a smooth transition from
mixed meter exercises to mixed meter literature, Mr. Johnston notates unison variations of familiar folksongs for the students to explore and enjoy.

A Newly-Discovered Star

These variations of familiar tunes set in a combination of steady-beat and unsteady-beat meters are very effective in helping students to understand and appreciate the vitality and energy that rhythmic variation can bring to pieces of music. They offer a more effective introduction to mixed meter than simply playing pieces originally composed in mixed meter, because the students know the original melodies so well. They can readily compare and contrast the differences between the originals and the variations.

Comparing and contrasting are important and well-respected modes of learning. They provide a natural road to self-discovery. We know and understand cold because we have experienced hot, and we have compared the differences. We understand fast because we have seen and experienced slow. Students playing the above variation will, very likely without conscious thought, compare and contrast it with the old, familiar "Twinkle, Twinkle Little Star," which is an integral part of their learned repertoire of songs. They are able to discover the true essence of mixed meter by comparing and contrasting old and new experiences. They are, once again, learning by doing, rather than by lecture.

Changing $3\frac{1}{4}^{\frac{1}{2}}$ Into a "Real" Time Signature

The students have by now mastered the concept and the performance of combining regular and irregular meter music. The only remaining step required before issuing a piece of music that incorporates this device is to change the time signature format to the one they will actually see in the literature. This needs to happen before such a piece is handed out.

What they know as $1\frac{1}{4}\,2$ will be seen in the literature as $\frac{3}{8}$.

What they know as $2\frac{1}{4}\,2$ will be seen in the literature as $\frac{5}{8}$.

What they know as $3\frac{1}{4}\,2$ will be seen in the literature as $\frac{7}{8}$.

What they know as $4\frac{1}{4}\,2$ will be seen in the literature as $\frac{9}{8}$.

In a very real sense, it is unfortunate that this last step must be taken. For most students, it adds a level of unnecessary confusion to the process. It can legitimately be argued that the most logical time signatures for this kind of music are the unique ones that these students have been introduced to by their teacher. Looking at the variation of "Twinkle, Twinkle Little Star" on the preceding page, it is undeniable that the quarter note is one count throughout the song. It is, therefore, logical in the students' minds that the bottom number of the time signatures should remain a "4" throughout the piece. In addition, all of the irregular meter measures do, indeed, have three-and-a-half counts in them. The most simple and logical time signature for those measures is $\frac{3}{4}\frac{1}{2}$. The variation as notated makes perfect sense to the students, although it is unusual and, perhaps, somewhat confusing to us. But if the students are "getting it," might it not be worth some temporary confusion on our parts?

It is interesting to imagine that, if these kinds of time signatures were commonly in use, students sightreading music that utilized them would know with a quick glance at the time signature how the music in those measures would be conducted. Seeing $1\frac{1}{4}\frac{1}{2}$, they would instantly know that the measure is going to be conducted in an elongated one. Seeing $2\frac{1}{4}\frac{1}{2}$, they would instantly know that the measure is going to be conducted in an unbalanced two. A measure of $3\frac{1}{4}\frac{1}{2}$ would symbolize an unbalanced three, and $4\frac{1}{4}\frac{1}{2}$ would be conducted in an unbalanced four. Time signatures of $\frac{3}{8}$, $\frac{5}{8}$, $\frac{7}{8}$, and $\frac{9}{8}$ cannot possibly claim such simplicity and logic.

Although the majority of students will not see printed literature that uses fractional time signatures, they do exist in more advanced literature. Nevertheless, teachers might consider introducing irregular and mixed meters in the way that has been demonstrated here. If the teaching of rhythm is to be effective and successful, it must be perceived by students to be simple and logical. After students have successfully completed a unit of study patterned on this one, they can then be shown the relationship between $3\frac{1}{4}\frac{1}{2}$ and the much more common $\frac{7}{8}$. Chances are good they will understand the mathematics involved, because they have already mastered the performance of it.

Once it is pointed out to students that traditional time signatures consist of whole numbers only, most middle school students competent in math can tell you that, in order to express $1\frac{1}{2}\!\!\!\!_4$ in a way that uses only whole numbers, both numbers must be multiplied by two.

$1\frac{1}{2}$ x 2 = **3**	$2\frac{1}{2}$ x 2 = **5**	$3\frac{1}{2}$ x 2 = **7**	$4\frac{1}{2}$ x 2 = **9**
4 x 2 = **8**	**4** x 2 = **8**	**4** x 2 = **8**	**4** x 2 = **8**

By the way, students should be taught that, when writing a traditional time signature on a staffless chalkboard or piece of paper, it should *not* be written as a fraction, as in $\frac{5}{8}$. The top and bottom numbers of time signatures have absolutely no mathematical relationship to each other. The line that appears to exist between them is simply the third line of the musical staff.

Once it is determined that a measure of music with a time signature of $\frac{7}{8}$, for example, is not in simple meter, the definition of the top and bottom numbers of that signature can be the same as the definition for compound meter (see page 187). The $\frac{7}{8}$ time signature means that there are the equivalent of seven eighth notes per measure. Because seven is an odd number, the individual beats in that measure cannot be the same length. One of them will be longer, the equivalent of three eighth notes, resulting in *irregular* meter and an *unsteady* beat.

After Mr. Johnston has taught his students to convert his unique, introductory time signatures to traditional ones, he ends the unit of study of irregular and mixed meters by notating additional familiar folksong materials, this time using both time signature formats, so that students can compare the differences.

Mary Had Two Mixed-Up Lambs

No. 2

It is interesting to note that if fractional time signatures like the ones in No. 1 on the preceding page were more commonly used, the sometimes confusing indication of (♪=♪) would not be necessary. The eighth notes would naturally be the same one-half count duration throughout, because the bottom number of the time signature is "4" throughout the entire piece.

Students enjoy playing these differently-flavored familiar songs. Because the melodies are technically so easy, they can concentrate fully on how the rhythm has changed the overall perception of the song. They can literally "get into the swing of the thing." They will likely approach unfamiliar mixed meter literature with the same vitality and interest.

Mr. Johnston's unit of study involving irregular meter and how it is used in mixed meter compositions has come to a successful conclusion. His students understand the derivation of irregular meter, how to perform it, and its effect upon the music. And they enjoy it! The students received a short lesson on the material at every rehearsal without fail, because it was an integral part of the teacher's daily written lesson plan. Each step in the process was presented as a logical extension of the previously mastered one. The daily exposure facilitated maximum retention of the material. We learn best those things we consistently do. Once again, the secret was in the planning.

Counting Irregular Meter

Simplicity has been an overriding mission of this book. When we introduce new concepts and skills to students, we need to strive to present the materials in the most logical and simple way possible. Our goal should be to get students to think as follows when being introduced to a new concept: "Well, of course. That makes perfect sense," rather than the all-too-common, "Huh?" Counting systems, being as important as they are to the process of rhythmic skill attainment, are no exception. They must make sense.

To help students gain complete confidence in their ability to understand rhythmic notation, there needs to be a set of what we might call "rhythm laws" that provide a solid foundation upon which students can base their knowledge. Unfortunately, these laws are often not clearly established and are sometimes actually false laws. We have discussed at length the fact that many of us mistakenly allow our students to falsely conclude that the whole note is exclusively music's symbol for the number four. With the advent of instruction in cut time, we inform them that the whole note is two counts. The students' rhythmic foundation becomes unstable, leaving them confused and puzzled. If the basic student-perceived fundamental law that says a whole note is always four counts can change, they wonder what else might change in the future. We have a duty to provide our students with a solid bedrock of unchangeable information upon which they can build, with absolute certainty, their understanding of rhythm theory. Rhythmically speaking, students need to be able *to count on certain things* -- pun intended.

- Only some whole notes are four counts and, when the whole note value changes , all note values change. You can count on it.
- Only some half notes are two counts, but all half notes are one-half as long as whole notes. That will never change. You can count on it.
- A whole note that is two counts is still a whole note. It will never be called by another name. Once a whole note, always a whole note. You can count on it.
- And many more unchangeable laws, like the one that follows, that students can always count on.

The Recommended Counting System

When it comes to counting systems, an unchangeable law that students ought to be able to rely upon with certainty was earlier stated this way: "Two rhythms that sound the same must use the exact same rhythm lyrics, no matter how they look on paper" (p. 177). To count the sound of triplets in one meter as *1-trip-let 2-trip-let* but in another as *1 2 3 4 5 6* is needlessly confusing and, simply stated, makes no sense to students. This was the reason it was suggested that triplets in compound 6/8 should not be counted in six unless triplets in 2/4 are also counted in six, which is highly unlikely. Our students need to be told that, if they sound like triplets, they are triplets, no matter how they are written, and they will all be counted with the same words. You can count on it!

208

For these reasons, the counting of the mixed meter example that follows is probably best avoided. The notes all sound exactly the same, but they have different lyrics, which invites confusion and, most likely, a long and involved explanation. We understand it, but it is difficult for students new to these concepts to understand why the half-count notes in the second measure appear to be getting one full count, given the counting of *1 2 3 4 5*.

Yes, we can explain that the notes that are counted *1 2 3 4 5* are really one-half count because we're saying their numbers twice as fast as we said the numbers in the first measure, but from an objective, student-centered point of view, how much sense does that really make? The longer and more involved the explanation required to clear up such an obvious discrepancy in the minds of students, the greater the number of students who will drop by the wayside. It's not that our explanations are not good ones. It just seems that very often, the longer the explanation, the less the understanding. Too many young learners are quick to say "I don't get it, so I don't want to think about it any more." We ought to strive, in so far as possible, to present rhythmic materials in such a way that there are no questions like the one above that need to be addressed.

The notes in this example all sound the same. They are all evenly spaced half-count notes. Our students need to be told that, if they sound like half-count notes, they are half-count notes, no matter how they are written, and they will all be counted with the same words. You can count on it! Basically speaking, students are going to understand this material far better if we can tell them that *all* half-count notes are counted as *1-&s* or *Du-des* or *Down-ups,* and so forth. Consistency, based on unchangeable rhythm laws, helps us to convince students that the entire system of counting rhythms is logical and immediately makes sense, no questions asked.

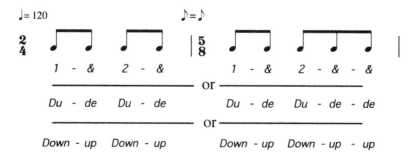

Irregular Meter and the Conductor's Baton

The above musical example is conducted, tapped, and felt in two beats to the measure throughout. The 5/8 measures are in an elongated, unbalanced two, but because of the tempo, they are without a doubt, in two. No one would conduct those measures in five. In my view, the way we conduct music such as this provides another reason why the 5/8 measures should not be counted in five. Music that is conducted in two needs to be counted in two. To students, that just makes sense. Counting and conducting should always be dynamically linked. Students need be able to see where rhythmic figures reside on the conductor's beat pattern. (See "Putting Rhythms Into Space" pages 132-142). The two separate groupings of three beamed eighth notes above are clearly on elongated conducting beat two. There is no conducting beat three, so there should be no counting word "three."

Closing Thoughts on Counting Systems in Irregular Meter

The counting system that is being advocated here is probably rather unconventional. That should not surprise anyone who has read this book from the beginning. Hopefully, you have come to expect the unexpected. We are, after all, encouraging you to look at rhythm through a new window.

As was stated before when discussing counting systems, my intention has not been to try to change the minds of those who are totally dedicated to their preferred systems. I have simply tried to point out some examples of what I perceive to be serious inconsistencies that occur all too often when we teach counting in irregular and mixed meters.

When we use different counting lyrics for the same sounds, we are being inconsistent. When the counting word "three" is on conducting beat two, we are being inconsistent. When we apply whole numbers to notes that are not whole counts, we are being inconsistent, and inconsistency leads to student doubt and confusion, neither of which is the desired outcome of instruction. No matter our preferred counting systems, we owe it to our students to avoid inconsistencies whenever possible.

Final Thoughts

My sixth grade band rehearsal started as any other, but it very soon became one of those wonderful, enlightening ones in which the teacher learned far more than any of the students. They were busy, quietly warming up. I was circulating among them, handing out a new piece. Suddenly Kevin, one of the less-able students in the class, shouted out a question loudly enough for everyone in the room to hear. Waving the new piece of sheet music in my direction, he asked, "Mr. Newell, how's this go?"

Everyone stopped playing. The room fell silent. I was basically speechless. I looked at him with a puzzled expression on my face, as a flood of memories swept over me. It occurred to me that I had not heard that annoying question for several years. How could I have forgotten it? It used to really irritate me whenever I heard it, and I heard it far more often than I care to reveal. As I was taking a couple of seconds to search for a suitable, informative, short, polite response, another student broke the silence. She took it upon herself to answer Kevin's question with a few, simple, succinct, well-chosen words. "What do you mean how's it go, Kevin? Ya' just *read* it!," she exclaimed with a touch of irritation in her voice. Perfect answer, Tricia. Thank you.

With that single, spontaneous student interaction, it dawned on me that something fantastic had occurred over time in my classroom. The great majority of the students in the room had become self-reliant readers of music. The idea of asking me how something goes never crossed their minds. They seemed as surprised as I that anyone would even ask such a question. It would never occur to any of them to ask their English teacher how a classroom reading assignment goes. When they got a reading assignment in English class, they just read it. If they had a problem with a word, they had been taught how to "sound it out." So why would they ask me how something goes when I handed out a new "reading assignment" in band? If they had a problem with a rhythm, they knew that it was their job to sound it out by counting it. Ya' just read it, Kevin.

What a significant change from my earlier days in the classroom. As a young teacher, I taught rhythm the way I was taught it, and my students were very often forced to rely on me for telling them how things went. That's because I had not provided them with the tools they needed to be self-sufficient, independent decoders of the rhythmic symbols they saw on the page. As I gradually grew in my understanding of how students learn rhythm and, therefore, how I needed to teach it, the students' attitudes about rhythm changed. Because they had been patiently guided through a carefully planned and executed sequence of rhythmic experiences, they knew that reading rhythm was their responsibility, and it was a responsibility that they accepted with confidence. They certainly didn't need my help to tell them how anything went.

Change Is Inevitable, But Seldom Easy

This book has encouraged you to look differently at some aspects of the teaching of rhythm, to think outside the 4/4 box. The problem with this idea is that many of us feel so very comfortable within the confines of that box. We relish the sense of security that its boundaries afford us. We know what the results are going to be when we teach from within it, because that is where our teachers stood when they taught us, and look how well we turned out! Plus, we cannot be sure what the future holds if we break down those walls and venture in a new, more open direction, even if it is one that holds the promise of helping students to arrive at the destination far sooner than we did. An unknown future, viewed from the present, can be a scary place. That great American philosopher, Yogi Berra, put it this way: "The trouble with the future is it ain't what it used to be." But it seems that many times, what used to be is not as good as what could have been. Change always involves some risk, but it is undeniably the fuel that drives progress. Change can be an invigorating challenge and a bountiful joy.

Human nature is generally not receptive to change, especially if it involves unconventional thinking and unknown results. Numerous visionary, creative, unconventional ideas relative to the teaching and learning of rhythm have been advanced in this book. The implication has been throughout that you might want to try some of these new ideas in your own teaching practice. Such a decision will undoubtedly require that you make some changes, and that is a decision that only you can make. Marilyn Ferguson, speaking of change, put it this way: "No one can persuade another to change. Each of us guards a gate of change that can only be opened from the inside. We cannot open the gate of another, either by agreement or by emotional appeal." We all need to decide for ourselves whether the possible outcomes are worth the taking of some new roads on our individual journeys toward our mutual destination of musically educated students.

Acknowledgments

Although only one person's name is listed as the author of this book, countless contributions of time, talent, and encouragement by others are what has made its publication possible. The author wishes to recognize and thank the following, among others too numerous to mention:

- **The Neil A. Kjos Music Company**, for its seventy-plus years of dedication to music education and, specifically, for its generous and unfailing support of this project.

- **John Knight**, **Ed Lisk**, and **Joe Manfredo**, for their willingness to read the manuscript and for their subsequent generous endorsements. The book has been made more readable and meaningful because of their questions and their suggestions.

- **Doug Beauchamp**, my cyber-friend. Doug and I have never met. He responded to a rhythm comment I made on a music website a few years ago, and we immediately realized we were both singing from the same hymnal. His willingness to read the manuscript during various stages of its writing, and his superb editing suggestions early on kept me focused on "keeping it simple."

- **Mary Ellen Huber**, my dear friend, a creative and talented elementary music specialist, who asked me to let her try these ideas with her third, fourth, and fifth grade general music classes. Her experiences with those students confirmed my belief that even very young students can gain a complete understanding of rhythm theory.

- **Dwight Oltman**, **Kristine Krejsa**, **Ellen Hansen-Ellis**, and **Susan Paxson**, all of whom read the manuscript at various stages during its development, and who encouraged me to finish it.

- And finally, **my wonderfully patient wife Judy**, who has heard about seven-count whole notes for so many years that she has probably wanted to scream whenever I have brought it up --- but she never did!

About the Author

David Newell taught music for thirty years in the public schools of Berea, Ohio. Additionally, he taught part-time in the Music Education Department at Baldwin-Wallace College for fifteen years. During his tenure as Director of Bands at Ford Middle School, Mr. Newell developed one of the exemplary band programs in the state and served as Chair of the Music and Art Departments. Chosen as one of the school district's first Consulting Teachers, he was responsible for guiding new music teachers through a three-year mentoring process.

In 1979, Mr. Newell received the Martha Holden Jennings Foundation's "Master Teacher" Award for Excellence in the Classroom. He also received the "Alumni Achievement" Award from Baldwin-Wallace College in 1987.

Mr. Newell earned his Bachelor of Music Education and Master of Arts in Education degrees from Baldwin-Wallace College and has taken postgraduate courses at Akron, Cleveland State, Kent State, and Northwestern Universities.

Also by David Newell:

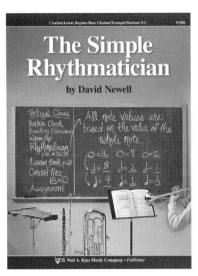

The Simple Rhythmatician is a unison, supplementary, young band book that is based 100% on the unique theoretical principles expressed in *Part Two* of **Teaching Rhythm: New Strategies and Techniques for Success**. The book is a *rhythm theory book,* but one with a significant difference. ***This is a theory book that students play.***

Students *read* rhythm theory, and they demonstrate their cognitive understandings as they complete worksheets and *write* both melodic and rhythmic compositions. But unlike other music theory books, this one goes a step beyond reading and writing. Young band students using this particular book also pick up their instruments and they *play* the theory as they are learning it. ***The theory comes alive through sound.*** This unison band method approach allows all of the students to immediately put theory into practice. Generally speaking, students learn what they *do* more profoundly than they learn what they read and write. The learning is in the doing.

Students are ready to begin *The Simple Rhythmatician* when they are secure in the performance of eighth notes in 2/4, 3/4, and 4/4 time.

Ed. W38 . . . . .9 Part Books, Score

Classic Christmas Carols for Band is a collection of 15 of the most popular and treasured Christmas carols presented in the unique *Kjos Total Option Scoring* format. Each part book contains all four choral voice parts, written in the playable range of each instrument, allowing for unlimited flexibility in instrumentation. Not only can these carols be performed in traditional full band arrangements, but they can be also performed as solos, duets, trios, quartets, and larger ensembles in absolutely any combination of instruments. Additionally, the full band or small ensemble can incorporate choir, and even the audience, to bring the holiday concert to an unforgettable grand finale.

Ed. W36 . . . . . 13 Part Books, Piano Accompaniment, Score

Classic Christmas Carols for Choir is published for SA Choir, Flexible Three-Part Choir, and SATB Choir, and may be used with or without the accompaniment of *Classic Christmas Carols for Band*. Many of the vocal parts have been given a traditional harmonization, while others have received a more modern treatment, resulting in a delightful variety of settings.

Ed. V90...SATB   **Ed. V91**... SA   **Ed. V92** ... 3-Part

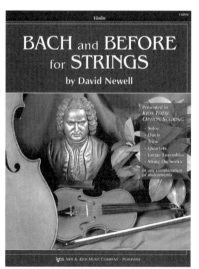

Bach and Before for Band and *Bach and Before for Strings* each contain a total of 19 chorales – 10 by Johann Sebastian Bach and 9 by his predecessors. Although both books feature the same 19 chorales, they cannot be combined for use in a full symphony orchestra setting. The chorales in the band book have been transposed to band-friendly keys and the chorales in the string book have been set in string-friendly keys. This has been done purposely, so that students can devote their full attention to *intonation* and *expressive phrasing*.

Both books are formatted in the *Kjos Total Option Scoring*. In every part book, all four of the original chorale voice parts – soprano, alto, tenor, and bass – are written in the playable range of each instrument, allowing for unprecedented flexibility in rehearsal strategies.

To get the maximum benefit out of these chorales, it is recommended that directors first have their ensembles learn just the soprano part, in unison, a few minutes every rehearsal, until it is played expressively by the full ensemble. This is followed by the alto part, the tenor part, and the bass part, each rehearsed and mastered in unison by the full ensemble. Then, for the first time, the chorale is played in four parts. The result is a highly expressive performance, because the director has taught all of the students how to play each part musically. *The students know the score as well as the teacher does.*

As each chorale voice is rehearsed in unison by the full ensemble, *intonation improves*. Every time an ensemble plays in unison, it is playing in several octaves simultaneously, and in-tune octaves are the basis of ensemble tuning. If the octaves are out-of-tune, it is impossible to tune a chord. *The more time spent playing in unison, the better the ensemble intonation.*

Bach and Before for Band
Ed. W34. . . . . . .12 Part Books, Piano Accompaniment, Score

Bach and Before for Strings
Ed. 110. . . . . .4 Part Books, Piano Accompaniment, Score

Please contact your favorite music store to purchase these books, or visit www.kjos.com for more information.